808.02

The
Author's
Toolkit

A Step-by-Step Guide to Writing and Publishing Your Book

REVISED EDITION

Mary Embree

Northern Plai~
Au~

ALLWORTH PRESS
NEW YORK

08 07 06 05 04 03   5 4 3 2 1

Published by Allworth Press
An imprint of Allworth Communications, Inc.
10 East 23rd Street, New York, NY 10010

Cover and interior design by Joan O'Connor
Page composition/typography by Integra Software Services, Pvt. Ltd., Pondicherry, India
ISBN: 1-58115-260-4
Library of Congress Cataloging-in-Publication Data

Embree, Mary, 1932-
The author's toolkit : a step-by-step guide to writing and publishing your book / Mary Embree.—Rev. ed.
p. cm.
Includes bibliographical references and index.
ISBN 1-58115-260-4
1. Authorship. 2. Authorship—Marketing. I. Title.

PN147.E43 2003
808'.02'02—dc21
2002156733

Printed in Canada

Contents

Preface

The approach I use in this book is unconventional. Maybe that's because I've spent so much time around writers of all kinds and written in various genres myself. For a number of years I worked in television production in positions ranging from assistant to the producer and script reader to staff researcher and writer. I've written educational videos, written and directed an independent documentary and a video for the California Youth Authority, and written scripts for television pilots and the 1980s TV series *This Is Your Life.*

During my years of working on sitcoms such as *Good Times, One Day at a Time,* and *Three's Company,* I learned timing, pacing, continuity, and plot construction. And I got an idea of what was funny and what was not. That was where I began to understand what a "hook" is. Even successful, highly paid writers don't score on every play, I discovered. Although you can learn certain techniques, writing isn't a science. It's a creative endeavor.

Over the past decade I have written three books, which have all been published, and have been working with other writers as a consultant, editor, teacher, and sounding board. While working with others, I noticed that certain questions came up again and again. To help these writers, I began writing booklets on basic composition and word usage, and on how to write query letters and prepare book proposals. I gave them to my clients and used them when I conducted workshops and seminars. Eventually I had written fifty or sixty pages of instructions and decided to use them in putting together this book.

I first published *The Author's Toolkit* myself. I knew that I could use it in my classes, give it to my clients, and sell it in workshops, seminars, and at book festivals. I had a thousand books printed, figuring they'd last me for at least five years. I sent out review copies to a few publications and, surprisingly, the book was reviewed in *Library Journal*. As a result of that review, orders started to pour in and within a few weeks my book was sold out and I had to have more copies printed.

Suddenly I had become a book publisher. It was fun for a while but the novelty wore off when I realized that I was spending too much time on paperwork, shipping, and such. I was having trouble finding enough time to take care of my clients. And I didn't have any time at all left over for my own writing. So in late 2001, I sent *The Author's Toolkit* and a proposal for a revised edition of it out to publishers and I was thrilled when Tad Crawford of Allworth Press called me and offered to publish it.

This edition is expanded and updated. Among other things, it contains a lot more about the writing process than the original book. Another plus about this edition is that it definitely benefits from being professionally edited by someone other than myself. I'm just not that objective. It's too easy to overlook my own mistakes. I love being on the other side of the fence—having *my* manuscript edited for a change. Allworth's Senior Editor Nicole Potter made excellent suggestions for improving the book, which I faithfully (and gratefully) followed. The changes she made, including rewording some of the sentences, resulted in greater clarity and readability of the manuscript.

I hope you will find this book helpful in your writing endeavors but that you will follow your own creative instincts when they differ from what you read here.

Although I have been called a book doctor, I would prefer to be considered a teacher. Amos Bronson Alcott, educator, philosopher, and the father of Louisa May Alcott, said, "The true teacher defends his pupils against his own personal influence. He inspires self-trust. He guides their eyes from himself to the spirit that quickens him. He will have no disciple."

—Mary Embree

Introduction

Do you love to write? Do you need to write? Would not writing pose a serious threat to your emotional well-being? To your mental health? Would you write even if you thought you might not be able to sell your work? Even if no one ever read it?

If you answered yes to any of those questions, this book is for you. It will give you some basic guidelines on writing nonfiction or a novel. It will give you some pointers on editing your own work and maybe help you to be a little more objective than you are now. It will tell you what you need to know to prepare a professional-looking manuscript and give you some advice on contacting the appropriate agent or publisher. It will also tell you what you need to do if you choose to publish your book yourself.

There is no guarantee that you will get a publishing contract even if you do everything that is recommended here. Many publishers have gone out of business or have merged with or sold out to larger publishers. The trend has been toward fewer publishers buying fewer manuscripts. Their inventory has been drastically reduced and most of them want a sure thing—or what they believe would be a sure thing. A new, unproven writer will need to have something outstanding in some way before a publisher will respond with anything more than a form letter of rejection. That is the bad news.

The good news is that, with the proper preparation, some sage advice, a little talent, and a whole lot of perseverance, you certainly have a chance of getting published. There have been some amazing success stories about first-time authors getting terrific publishing contracts and turning out bestsellers. It is my belief that if you have ever written anything—business proposals, technical manuals, poetry, or even a daily journal—you can learn to write a book. Talent can't be taught but craft can.

Any story worth telling, any lesson worth teaching, and any idea worth expressing is worth writing about. And if you can tell, teach, or express your thoughts well, you can write a book. So if you really, really want to write, what's stopping you?

Maybe it seems to be too daunting a task—so many words, so many pages—and you don't even know where to begin. You might be one of those writers who ponders the nuance of every word and takes a long time to get her thoughts down on paper. Well, take heart. In his book *Half a Loaf,* Franklin P. Adams wrote, "Having imagination, it takes you an hour to write a paragraph that, if you were unimaginative, would take you only a minute. Or you might not write the paragraph at all." Consider the possibility that you may be an excellent writer who simply needs to sit down and write.

You may worry about how to make your book interesting, how to organize it and put it together coherently. When you have completed the final draft, you may not have a clue as to how to find an agent to represent it or a company to publish it. If you feel that way, you are not alone. Many first-time authors feel overwhelmed at the beginning. Even though I had done a lot of writing before, when it came to writing a book, I had all of those fearful feelings—until I learned the process.

Both editing and writing require large doses of concentration, discipline, passion, dedication, and integrity. Although writing can be enormously gratifying, good writing isn't easy, at least not for me or any of the other writers I know. And the necessary self-editing of your work requires great attention to detail.

There are some common pitfalls that I have noticed through working with hundreds of writers both individually as my clients and in groups at writers' conferences and in the classes I teach. I will explain how to avoid them and I'll give you some valuable principles you can apply both to your writing and self-editing.

Whether or not you are working on a book right now, write every day. It has been said that if you do a thing for twenty-one days in a row, it becomes a habit. In *The Artist's Way,* Julia Cameron advises writing three pages every morning. Those pages don't have to lead to a book, they can be about anything. The important thing is that you establish a pattern of writing.

There are many paths you can take to authorship and I suggest you take as many of them as you can. Attend writers' conferences, book festivals, seminars, and writing classes. Join organizations where you can network with and get inspired by other writers. Subscribe to writers' magazines and newsletters. Buy books on writing and study them. Let them become your bedtime reading. Become familiar with the writing process and learn the rules. Then have the courage to break a few of those rules when they get in the way of what you want to say.

Chapter 1

In the Beginning Is the Idea

Ideas are to literature what light is to painting.
—PAUL BOURGET

The idea always comes first. You have to know what you want to write about before you start writing. Write a short blurb that describes the book. Assign it a working title that will identify it. That will be the name you will also put on the folders you create for the project, such as Research, News Clips, Bibliography, Illustrations, Notes, Endorsements, Biographical Information, Character Descriptions, or any other material you gather or create that relates to your proposed book.

The concept sometimes changes. It may grow, improve, or maybe even move in a different direction from that which you had originally planned.

Is it hard to get started? Samuel Johnson said, "What is written without effort is in general read without pleasure." And Molière lamented, "I always do the first line well, but I have trouble doing the others." So, see? You're in good company.

Don't worry if you can't figure out what that first page, first paragraph, first sentence should be. You don't have to know that now. You might find after you have written fifteen chapters that your book really starts at chapter 5 and you can throw away chapters 1, 2, 3, and 4, or plug them in somewhere else.

GETTING STARTED

Knowing how and where to begin can be the most agonizing part of the process. Many writers have their worst case of writer's block before they ever put a word on the page. As they sit and stare at the blank sheet of paper or computer screen, they may wonder why on earth they ever chose to write anyway. Well, there are some tricks to get you going, to help you get *something* down on paper before the day is over.

If you plan to write nonfiction, you could start by explaining what kind of book it is, why you are writing it, and who will benefit from reading it. If you can convince yourself that there is a very good reason for your book, you'll probably have no trouble going on from there.

If you are writing a novel, explain what the story is about. Then describe your main character and put him into a scene that reveals his personality. Where is he? What is she doing? What is he feeling? Is there something compelling about your protagonist? As important as plot is, most of the best novels are character driven. You must know your protagonist intimately so that you will understand why she makes the decisions she does, why he is angry, how far she will go to get her way, or what he is willing to do to get ahead. What are the limits? Where will your protagonist draw the line? Your characters tell the story and they will take you to exotic and mysterious places you may never have dreamed you'd go. After you do this exercise, if you feel that you have an interesting protagonist and a story that must be told, it will be easy—well, easier—to continue.

In his book *Double Your Creative Power,* S. L. Stebel suggests writing a book jacket for your novel, thinking of it "as a kind of preview of coming attractions." I advise the nonfiction authors I work with to become familiar with the book-proposal format or even to prepare a proposal as soon as the idea for a book occurs to them. There's probably nothing more disappointing to an author than writing a whole manuscript and finding out it doesn't have a chance of getting published. The research that must be done to write a proposal would turn up that information. Another reason to study the book-proposal format is to help you focus on your subject and organize your work.

What if you have done all of the above and you are still staring at a blank page wondering what that first sentence of your book will be, the one that you know is only the *most* important line in the entire book? This is not the time to concern yourself with writing the perfect opening sentence. That may come to you later. The important thing is just to relax and start writing. *Get something* onto the page.

If you think that you still aren't on track, it may be time to disengage your conscious mind. Take a walk, wash the car, mow the lawn, plant some flowers—do anything that shifts your brain into neutral—and stop worrying about it. Then tonight, before you go to sleep, get very comfortable and relaxed and tell yourself that tomorrow when you wake up you will know exactly where to begin. Convince yourself that during the night your subconscious mind will sort it all out and next day you will approach that blank page virtually exploding with creativity. Sometimes this works so well for me that my subconscious mind won't let me wait until morning. It wakes me up in the middle of the night with the answer. I turn on the light, get out the pen and paper that I keep in my nightstand drawer, and write it down in detail. There are times when ideas flash as urgently as lights on an ambulance, and I must get up, turn on my computer, and start typing feverishly. I love it when that happens.

PLANNING YOUR BOOK

Do an outline or write chapter headings and a short paragraph on what's in each chapter. Some writers put this information on small index cards and arrange them on a table. They can then see the whole book at a glance and rearrange the chapters if necessary. If you are writing a novel, write character sketches too. Get to know the information, people, and events that are involved in your story so that you can confidently introduce them to the reader. Once you have a plan, a road map of where you are going, you are not likely to drift off, become lost, or encounter writer's block.

Have a clear idea of what you want to say and then develop your concept along those lines. But don't be rigid. Let it flow like water in a stream, following its own natural course. Unleash your creativity; you can always cut and edit later. Make it interesting. If it interests you, it probably will interest others.

WRITE A ONE-SENTENCE DESCRIPTION

To help yourself focus on your subject, write one sentence or a sentence fragment that describes your book. Check best-seller lists to see how they do this. Here are some examples. (F is for fiction; NF is for nonfiction.)

Who Moved My Cheese? by Spencer Johnson. [NF] The author tells how to manage change by using the parable of mice in a maze.

Single & Single by John Le Carré. [F] An English banker and a Russian mobster are involved in murder, bribery, betrayals, and other forms of villainy.

The Greatest Generation by Tom Brokaw. [NF] Stories of men and women who lived through the Depression and World War II.

Self Matters by Phillip C. McGraw. [NF] A self-improvement expert tells how to "create your life from the inside out."

Blues for All the Changes by Nikki Giovanni. [F] A collection of intensely personal poems on sex, politics, and love "among Black folk."

Fast Food Nation by Eric Schlosser. [NF] How the practices of the junk-food industry led to a nation of overweight and unhealthy people.

The Corrections by Jonathan Franzen. [F] The story of a dysfunctional family living in the Midwest in the late twentieth century.

******

There isn't any single way to explain what a book is about. But the above will give you an idea of how you could describe yours. Writing these one-sentence descriptions will help you with the writing process by focusing your ideas and sharpening your point of view. This exercise will also help you later, when you are out there marketing your book. There will be more about this in chapters 11 and 12, on book proposals and query letters, respectively.

For most of us who possess the soul of a writer, there are book ideas that call us, begging us to write them and bring them out of obscurity. I think it would be sad to reach the end of our days and realize with regret that we never did get around to writing that book—the one that tugged at our heart for so many years.

What is the book that calls to you? Is it nonfiction? Are there valuable lessons you could teach? Is there important information you could share? Is it a family history or an autobiography that generations of relatives who come after you would treasure? Is it your poetry that springs from deep within your heart that you've never really shared? Is it a novel that is trying to get your attention? Are there voices inside your brain that long to be heard, voices that only you can unsilence? Are there fascinating characters only you can bring to life? Will you let them languish mutely within the prison of your mind or turn them loose upon the world to tell their story?

When you take it one word at a time, it isn't so intimidating. And, after all, that is the only way you *can* write it.

Chapter 2

Research

When you steal from one author, it's plagiarism; if you steal from many, it's research.

—Wilson Mizner

No matter what you are writing about, the likelihood is that you will need to do some research on the subject. If you are writing nonfiction, research is essential. No matter how well you know your subject, your memory isn't perfect and even if it were there are changes that take place all the time that may make your knowledge outdated. You will have to be sure that your information is accurate, current, and has not already been written about in the way you intend to write it.

Even if you are writing a novel, there is likely to be information you will need. For example, suppose your protagonist is a cardiologist. You will need to know something about heart problems, surgical procedures, hospital protocol, and so forth. If the action in your novel takes place in Hong Kong, you will have to know enough about the geography, climate, customs, people, and laws to make your story feel authentic. It helps if you've been to Hong Kong but if you haven't been there recently and your story is set in the present time, you'll need to find out what it's like there now. There have been a lot of political changes in Hong Kong in the past few years.

You must be accurate about dates, the spelling of names, historical events, recent developments in your subject field, and on and on. The list is endless. The integrity of your research can make you look like an expert or like a novice.

Where do you find all this information? Fortunately for writers, the information highway has been repaved and many more lanes have been added. Here are the major ways to find the data you need.

THE INTERNET

Where we once had to get out of our house or office and go to the library, we can now get just about any information we need over the Internet. There is a caveat, however, to getting your facts that way. Not all of the information is unbiased and accurate. You will have to do the research necessary to check out your sources. And there isn't a friendly librarian sitting inside your computer who will help you through the maze of Web sites and tell you what to click on. You still have to know exactly what you are looking for and where to find it, and you must know the integrity of the source. Misinformation is worse than no information at all.

When you are gathering information or doing fact checking, be sure that the Web sites you go to are reputable. For instance, when I was doing research for my book on smoking, I checked out the American Lung Association, The National Cancer Society, and The American Heart Association Web sites. I went to the Web sites of the U.S. Department of Health and Human Services and the *New England Journal of Medicine* for reports of recent health studies on the effects of smoking. I didn't bother with tobacco companies because it's been proven that they lie and mislead.

When I wanted information on copyrights, I went directly to the U.S. Copyright Office Web site (*www.copyright.gov*). There I found up-to-date information, as well as copyright forms I could download. In updating my information for this revised edition of *The Author's Toolkit*, I discovered that the fee to register literary works (using Form TX) did not go up in June 2002 as expected. It was still $30.

THE PUBLIC LIBRARY

You could call the librarian of your local library and ask her to locate, copy, and send the information you are seeking to you.

However, libraries are so understaffed now that such services may no longer be available. You might have to go to the library to look things up yourself. But sometimes it's very nice—and inspiring—to get out of your office or house and go sit among the books. There is nothing like the quiet, stimulating energy of a library.

The librarians will teach you how to use the card file to locate what you need in the library and how to use their computer for researching, if you don't already know how to do so. There may be reference books in the library that you can't get on the Internet. For instance, *Literary Market Place* (*LMP*) has a Web site you can go to, but if you are not a paid subscriber, only a small portion of the information that is in its huge annual reference book is available to you. You probably wouldn't want to subscribe, because both the printed versions of the book and the online subscriptions are very expensive.

Usually you can access R. R. Bowker's *Books in Print* and *Forthcoming Books* on the library's computer. When you start doing research for your book proposal, these lists and *LMP* will be essential.

There are many other sorts of research materials available in libraries, such as microfiche of newspapers, clippings and art files, special collections, and back issues of magazines.

SPECIALIZED LIBRARIES

Many universities, medical centers, and corporate offices have extensive libraries. Some of them may require you to be connected with the institution in some way before they let you use them, but not all of them have those restrictions. Many of these libraries have books that are not available in a public library. You may find that their libraries are also more up-to-date and carry books, journals, and research papers on subjects that relate to what you are writing.

As I have written books, booklets, and articles on health issues, I have found medical libraries to be invaluable. When I was doing research for a book I was writing on smoking, I used the library at St. John's Regional Medical Center in Oxnard, California. The librarian helped me locate some recent studies that had been done all over the world on the health effects of smoking. Through this research I discovered that male and female addictions to tobacco are different, as are the difficulties that each sex faces in quitting smoking. I also found studies that showed the alarming health consequences of smoking for women, their pregnancies, fetuses, and small children. In 1994 these facts and statistics were virtually unknown to the public as well as to most medical doctors. Even though I had just completed the training to become a stop-smoking facilitator with the American Lung Association and I had all of their literature, I hadn't come across this information.

Instead of writing a general how-to-quit-smoking book, I focused on girls and women. I put together my book proposal and found a literary agent who was eager to represent me. Two publishers made offers and I chose the one with the larger advance. At that point I had only written three chapters. I chose not to spend the time writing the entire book until I knew that I could sell it. I didn't finish writing the book until after the publishing contract was signed and I had gotten the first half of my advance. The book was published the following year by WRS Group, a company that was owned by a medical doctor. The company chose the title: *A Woman's Way: The Stop-Smoking Book for Women.* From that book, which was sold mostly through bookstores, I spun off two other works: *The Stop-Smoking Program for Women*, to be used by therapists in the field, and a booklet called *The Stop-Smoking Diet for Women.* Both were published by Health Edco, an imprint of WRS Group, and sold mainly to hospitals, women's clinics, nursing associations, and doctors in private practice. The twenty-eight-page diet booklet sold better than the book.

That book would never have been written—or published—if I had not done the research and found information that had not been written about in a book before.

REFERENCE BOOKS

The New York Public Library Desk Reference contains a wealth of information on just about any subject you can think of. On its cover it states, "The complete resource for quick answers to all your questions." I think that is a bit of an overstatement. I can think of a few questions it won't answer. But it does contain an amazing amount of information. Of course, you can't expect it to go into detail on so many entries. However, if you don't need details, just a quick answer, this reference is excellent.

If you have the printed edition of the *Encyclopaedia Britannica* and it is recent, that's great. It is still considered by most experts to be the best encyclopedia available. If not, you can get it and other encyclopedias on CDs, which are considerably less costly than the printed versions. Again, it is essential to have a recently published encyclopedia. The information you need may not be in an older issue or may be out of date. Most encyclopedias publish a yearbook with updated information and it is a good idea to get it so that you can keep current.

It is imperative for a writer to have an unabridged dictionary in addition to a desk dictionary. Among desk dictionaries, I like the "college" dictionaries published by Houghton Mifflin and Random House. *The Oxford American Dictionary of Current English*, published by Oxford University Press is also excellent. Again, make sure you have a recent edition. Technology is changing so fast that dictionaries are out of date even before they are published. Many dictionaries that came out prior to 1997, both desk and unabridged types, do not contain the words *Internet*, *Web site*, and many technological words that are now in common usage. There is more on this subject in chapter 7.

A book of synonyms and antonyms is helpful if you find yourself using the same word over and over again. We all have pet words and usually don't even realize it. A thesaurus will help you find new words and different ways to say the same thing. And that will certainly make your writing more interesting. The books I particularly like are *Roget's Thesaurus* and Funk & Wagnalls *Standard Handbook of Synonyms, Antonyms and Prepositions*. The Funk & Wagnalls book was first published in 1914 under the title of *English Synonyms and Antonyms*. The first edition of Roget's was published in 1852. Of course, both of these books are updated and reissued every few years but it isn't as important to have a recent issue of a thesaurus as it is of a dictionary.

There's a wealth of information of all sorts in *The World Almanac*, *The Information Please Almanac*, and other books of this kind. As an example of the kind of information you may find in an almanac, a recent edition of *The World Almanac and Book of Facts* contained an article on the transition of power in Hong Kong when China regained control after 156 years of British rule. Since almanacs come out with new editions every year, they will have more up-to-date information than some encyclopedias.

Another reference book of this type is *The Cambridge Factfinder* published by Cambridge University Press. It contains a "collection of bits of information for use in the home, at school, or in the office" and claims to contain more facts than any other book of its kind—over 180,000. The book is divided into what they call "broad areas of knowledge" with sections on the universe, the Earth, the environment, natural history, human beings, history, human geography, society, religion and mythology, communications, science and technology, arts and culture, knowledge (academic study), and sports and games.

Research is tricky, and it is hard to define what a fact actually is, because there are facts about fictions and fictions about facts. *The Oxford English Dictionary* defines a fact as "Something that has really occurred or is actually the case; something certainly known to be of this character; hence a particular truth known by actual observation or authentic testimony, as opposed to what is merely inferred, or to a conjecture or fiction; a datum of experience, as opposed to the conclusions which may be based upon it."

Good research is important. If you are ever called to explain how you got your information, it's comforting to be able to cite a source to show that you didn't make up your facts.

REFERENCE BOOKS SPECIFIC TO YOUR SUBJECT

If you write regularly on historical subjects, medicine, alternative health, animals, or whatever, it's a good idea to accumulate reference books on these subjects. For example, if you were writing articles or a book having to do with health, you might need a medical dictionary, a family medical guide, or books on nutrition, pharmaceuticals, herbal medicines, and various forms of natural healing. If you were writing a mystery novel involving international intrigue, you might want to get books on spycraft, or on the CIA, the KGB, and other supersecret government agencies throughout the world.

Here is another area in which R. R. Bowker's *Books in Print* would be helpful. Their books are listed by subject matter as are those on Amazon.com. You can also check the books available in libraries and bookstores. They are placed on the shelves in sections devoted to each subject: mysteries, psychology, computers, etc.

Bookstore clerks and librarians can help you find what you need and may even be able to recommend specific books.

NEWSPAPERS, MAGAZINES, AND JOURNALS

Keep up with what is happening in the world on a daily basis. Subscribe to a newspaper, preferably a major one such as the *Washington Post*, *Wall Street Journal*, *New York Times*, or *Los Angeles Times*. They may not, however, be unbiased in their reporting, so be aware that you will still have to check your facts. Also subscribe to magazines and journals in your field. They will have more current information on your particular subject than other sources. They, too, may contain organizational bias, so it would be wise not to rely on them alone. *Publishers Weekly* and *Library Journal* are excellent resources. They review thousands of books a year, most of them new. You can keep up with what is happening in the world of book publishing and learn what kinds of books are most popular.

ORGANIZATIONS

Join organizations that are formed to bring together people with similar interests, and try to attend their meetings regularly. There is no way to overemphasize the importance of networking with people in the field you are writing about. They are a valuable source of information, inspiration, and assistance. You will also find out who publishes the kind of book you are writing and maybe even get a referral to an agent or publisher by a member who has been published. You will benefit from the research others in your field have done. See the list of organizations for writers under Resources, in the back of this book. To find local organizations, you could go to your Yellow Pages. They may be listed under various categories like "Associations," "Clubs," "Social Service Organizations." The Internet is also a good way to find specific organizations.

Seven years ago, I formed an organization called Small Publishers, Artists & Writers Network (SPAWN), because I couldn't find anything like it. I wanted to join an association where authors, graphic designers, editors, literary agents, publishers, and others interested in producing books came together. At our very first meeting a medical doctor who was writing and self-publishing a book met a professional graphic designer who ended up designing the doctor's book cover. We have found so many ways not only to work together but to learn from each other. It is really gratifying, too, to be around other people with interests similar to your own.

EXPERTS AND OTHER AUTHORS

When you need expert advice, go to someone who knows the field and subject well. It could take you hours to get the answer to a question through other forms of research when you might be able to contact experts who will answer your question in a matter of minutes. Most of the time this can be done on the phone and you can record the conversation (with their permission).

Reference books should be kept in your home or office library and replaced (or added to) each time a new edition comes out. Having information at your fingertips when you need it can be a real time-saver.

Researching can be very time-consuming when most of us would really rather be writing, but it can make the difference between producing an authoritative, informed, interesting book, and one that is merely mediocre. It can also, as in my case, make the difference between a book that has a good chance of finding a publisher and one that doesn't have a prayer.

A word of caution: be sure that you don't quote directly from any book without giving attribution to the author and getting permission from the publisher. Recently, two highly esteemed historians were caught quoting other authors extensively without using quotation marks or attributing the writing to the original author. It caused such a stir that both of these historians, whose books were regularly on best-sellers' lists, lost much of their credibility. Their reputations were tarnished if not ruined.

Plagiarism is probably the worst transgression an author can be accused of. Well, maybe being boring is the worst, but plagiarism is the ugliest. Also, without permission to use copyrighted works, you open yourself up to potential lawsuits. If you have any doubts about what you can and cannot use, consult an attorney who is knowledgeable in that area. There is more about this in chapter 19.

Chapter 3

Assemble Your Tools

Give us the tools and we will finish the job.
—WINSTON CHURCHILL,
BBC RADIO BROADCAST, FEBRUARY 9, 1941

You may feel that the only tools you need to write a book are a pen and a pad of paper. And that may be so. But if you want to be accurate and informed, you will need books for research. If you want to be able to write and edit quickly, you will need a word processor or a computer. If you wish to send your manuscript out to an agent or publisher, it must be typewritten or printed. If you use a computer, you will need a good printer.

In the 1800s, Thomas Carlyle said, "Man is a tool-using animal. . . . Without tools he is nothing, with tools he is all." He wasn't referring to writers but he could have been. Because without some basic tools, your book remains an idea in your head, incomplete, unrealized, and unrecorded.

At any stage in your writing you can assemble your tools, but the best time to start getting them together is before you begin the job. Think of how it would be if the only planning you did for painting your living room were to buy the paint and the paintbrush. You would soon find that you needed tools to open the paint can and to stir the paint with. After you started painting, you'd discover that you needed a drop cloth so that you wouldn't ruin the floor. And you might have to stop and spackle the nail holes before you continued.

Planning ahead and assembling all the tools you needed would have helped the process move along faster and more smoothly. The same is true for writing.

Here's a list of some tools to consider getting, with a box for you to check off each one as you acquire it. Keep everything you need close by—in the same room, if possible—so that you don't have to get up and go to another room to use them. Some you may not need or be able to get right now, and some you will already have.

EQUIPMENT

❏ A computer (with a monitor), word processor, or electric type-writer (preferably a correcting one)

❏ A laser or inkjet printer

❏ A desk, tabletop, or flat area that is for your exclusive use

❏ A good, supportive, comfortable chair on casters, so you can move it around easily

❏ A file cabinet or portable file box, so you can keep your rough drafts, notes, and research information in order

❏ A telephone

❏ A fax

❏ A scanner, so you can scan photos and illustrations that you wish to include in your book

❏ Good lighting

BOOKS

❏ An unabridged dictionary

❏ A desk dictionary

❏ A thesaurus

❏ A book of quotations

❏ An encyclopedia, either in print or on a computer disk

❏ Strunk and White's *The Elements of Style*

❏ *The Chicago Manual of Style*

❏ This year's edition of *Writer's Market*

❏ Any other reference books that will be of help in your particular writing project

SUPPLIES

❑ Paper: notepads and typing/computer paper
❑ Red pens to mark corrections and changes on your printed pages
❑ Black or blue pens for jotting down notes
❑ Yellow highlighter pens
❑ An extra ink or toner cartridge for your printer
❑ Computer disks to save your work on
❑ Staplers, staple removers, scissors, paper clips, scotch tape, etc.

Make a list of all the tools you think you will need and get them before you start writing. Not only will it save you time in the future, it will put you in the right frame of mind to write and could assuage that bad habit of most writers: procrastination.

That blockbuster novel may be germinating inside your brain at this very moment. You just could be a creative genius. You might have enormous talent—far bigger than anyone would ever guess. But to get your ideas down on paper in a presentable form you will have to be more than an accomplished author—you must also be a good craftsman. You still need the tools of the trade. They are of the utmost importance in your ability to finish the job.

YOUR TIME

You need to not only gather your tools and set up your workspace, you need to organize your time so that you can spend an hour or more each day writing. Once you get going, you may find that you are just getting warmed up in an hour. Then you may want to change your daily schedule or even your lifestyle so that you can fit in a three-hour writing period each day. That isn't easy to do if you are a busy stay-at-home parent of preschoolers or a business executive who works long hours. But those who are bitten hard by the writing bug somehow find the time. One writer I know gets up at four in the morning and gets in two or three hours of writing before her husband and children wake up. Another has a working space in his garage, where he goes after dinner and writes until bedtime. Establishing a routine is very helpful but if that is not possible, then write whenever you get a chance, even if it's only notes to elaborate on later.

It takes dedication and perseverance to write a book. How you prepare yourself depends on whether you are a serious writer or a hobbyist. Which one are you?

PREPARE YOURSELF

If your goal is to become a professional writer, you may need to brush up on your English or composition skills. You already know how to speak, to read, and to write, and maybe how to use a computer. But to become a really good writer you must understand grammar, word usage, parts of speech, sentence structure, spelling, punctuation, and all the other principles of composition. You probably were introduced to all this in school, but maybe you weren't really paying much attention. Some information on those subjects you will find in chapters 4 and 7, The Rules of Writing and Editing Principles, respectively. You may need only to be reminded of what you learned in your English courses. However, if you feel you are lacking in some area of writing, it would be a good idea to take some classes.

You can learn a great deal through books. The best one I can think of for writers at all levels of their profession is *The Elements of Style* by Strunk and White. However, just as no driver's training manual could turn a person into a good driver, no book or manual can turn you into a good writer. A person may know theoretically how to drive but he still has to get behind the wheel and do a lot of driving if he is to learn to drive well. And a writer will have to do a lot of writing to become a good writer. In writing, practice doesn't make perfect, because writing has no measure for perfection, but practice will surely make you a better writer.

What writing implement should you use? Whatever works best for you. A woman writer I know who was a touch-typist and could type fast still wrote all of her first drafts in longhand. She said, "I can be more creative when I can feel my ideas flow from my brain, through my fingers, into the pencil and spread out onto the paper."

Many seasoned writers still write their first draft longhand. Another writer told me he wrote with a pencil so that he could erase and make corrections. Soon he realized that he was erasing stuff that was better than his "corrections." After that he wrote with a pen and drew a line through the words he was replacing. Later, he began to write incomplete sentences longhand and then fleshed them out when he typed them up. When he graduated from his old IBM Selectric to the computer, he discovered he could compose right at the keyboard with no loss of creativity. Now he almost never writes anything in longhand. He says that he can type much faster than he writes. "When I'm in a creative rush, my ideas are like butterflies. When I use a computer, I can get my thoughts down on paper quickly, before they fly away and settle upon the next idea."

If you like to think out loud, you may be more comfortable talking into a tape recorder and having someone transcribe it for you. Now you can even dictate your book directly to disk on your computer with speech recognition software. Then you can print your first draft and start editing and refining it.

Chapter 4

The Rules of Writing

"Fool!" said my muse to me, "look in thy heart, and write."

—SIR PHILIP SIDNEY, *ASTROPHIL AND STELLA*

Think of your proposed book as a story. No matter what you are writing—a how-to or self-help book, an autobiography or a novel— you should have a story in mind: a beginning, a middle, and an end. There must be a basic concept, continuity, and logical transitions from one paragraph to the next and one chapter to the next.

If you have not yet decided exactly what your subject is, just start writing. Don't stop and edit the first two pages again and again before you go on. Keep going until your book idea comes into focus. Once it does, prepare an outline. If it is nonfiction, write chapter headings and a paragraph or two about what you plan to cover in each chapter. If it is a novel, write about the story. Tell sequentially everything that is going to happen and put this information into a chapter outline. Keep advancing the storyline and keep it simple. At this point, write quickly, concentrating on the story not on how you write it. Also write character sketches, describing all of the major ones in great detail. You may never use these descriptions in the book but you will understand your characters so well that you will know what they will and won't do. If your plot is character driven, as it should be, your story will probably change from your original plan. Don't worry about this for now.

WRITE FROM THE HEART

Whatever you are writing, write with passion. Whether it is a mystery novel or a how-to book, you must be enthusiastic about your subject or you will have trouble making it interesting to a reader. If you write a book simply because you think that it will sell, the process itself will not be rewarding and you will probably end up with a dull book. And dull books usually don't sell very well. Thomas Carlyle said, "If a book come from the heart, it will contrive to reach other hearts; all art and authorcraft are of small amount to that."

In his book *On Writing Well,* William Zinsser states, "Ultimately the product that any writer has to sell is not the subject being written about, but who he or she is." Your zeal, integrity, and warmth will draw a reader into your book, not hard facts and cold statistics.

Sidney Sheldon advises, "Write out of a passion, a caring, a need. The rest will follow."

IF YOU WOULD WRITE, READ

Read works that inspire you, excite you, enlighten, entertain, or surprise you—books that touch your feelings. Read books that are quoted often, like the Bible, the works of Shakespeare, and John Donne. Read the classics, the current best-sellers, and any books that may be a lot like the one you are writing. In *The Writing Life,* author Annie Dillard said, "[The writer] is careful of what he reads, for that is what he will write."

Whenever I am editing a manuscript for a book, I go out and buy a book that is in some way similar to the one I am working on. I focus on current best-sellers, because they indicate trends in reader tastes and interests. The book becomes my evening reading. I study it, noting how the author approached his subject, what he wrote on the first page. If it is a how-to book, I notice how the chapters are organized and how the information is explained. If it is a novel, I look at how the author has developed the story, what her characters are like, and how they are described. Then, as I go through the client's manuscript, making my little notes in red pen, I know that I am not going by training and instinct alone. I have a better understanding of what needs to be fixed and why because I have seen examples of good writing in books that are currently selling in that genre. That is an added value that I never charge for because it contributes to my education as well.

With every book I read, I learn something new. I also learn a great deal about my own writing through editing other writers. It's so much easier to see other people's mistakes. We get used to our own and either don't recognize them as mistakes or become protective of them.

KEEP IT SIMPLE

Walt Whitman wrote, "The art of art, the glory of expression and the sunshine of the light of letters, is simplicity." Simplicity does not mean the lack of complexity. It doesn't mean "talking down" to the reader. It may mean using smaller and simpler vocabulary, though, because that helps make the message clearer and more focused. And what is your point in writing, to show off your enormous vocabulary or to get your ideas across?

In Stephen King's autobiographical book *On Writing,* he says, "One of the really bad things you can do to your writing is to dress up the vocabulary, looking for long words because you're maybe a little bit ashamed of your short ones." In *The Art of Fiction,* John Gardner states, "A huge vocabulary is not always an advantage. Simple language . . . can be more effective than complex language, which can lead to stiltedness or suggest dishonesty or faulty education."

Replace polysyllabic words with words of one or two syllables. Break up long sentences. Turn them into two or three shorter ones. Greater clarity will be the result. Long words and complex sentences tend to be confusing and murky. Sentences that are difficult to read and understand will turn away a reader. Usually such sentences contain several thoughts and ideas and become too involved to be understood easily. Remember always that our goal is to write books people will enjoy reading. As Flannery O'Connor said, "You may write for the joy of it, but the act of writing is not complete in itself. It has its end in its audience."

Simplifying our writing is not just a modern concept. It is true that books are now competing with television, whose shows are often only a half hour long, and even that half hour is riddled with commercial interruptions. It might be that people really don't have as long an attention span as they once did. But the idea of aspiring to clear, simple, and concise writing did not evolve as an outcropping of the TV era. This principle has been around for a very long time. In 1580 Michel Eyquem de Montaigne wrote, "I want to be seen here in my simple, natural, ordinary fashion, without straining or artifice; for it is myself that I portray. . . . I am myself the matter of my book." In the nineteenth century, Leo Nikolaevich Tolstoy stated, "there is no greatness where there is not simplicity, goodness, and truth."

The most powerful writing is that which flows naturally, expressing the thoughts and feelings of the author in a clear, direct, and honest way. Get rid of the clutter in your writing as you would your old, outdated clothes. Clean out the closet of your mind and let the sunlight and fresh air in.

ADJECTIVES, ADVERBS, AND QUALIFIERS

An adjective is any of a class of words used to modify a noun by limiting, qualifying, or specifying. It is distinguished by having comparative and superlative endings like *-able, -ous, -er, -est*. To quote from *The Elements of Style,* "Write with nouns and verbs, not with adjectives and adverbs. The adjective hasn't been built that can pull a weak or inaccurate noun out of a tight place . . . it is nouns and verbs, not their assistants, that give good writing its toughness and color."

An adverb is distinguished by the ending *-ly* or by functioning as a modifier of verbs or clauses, adjectives or other adverbs or adverbial phrases, such as *very, well,* and *quickly.* Stephen King says, "I believe the road to hell is paved with adverbs, and I will shout it to the rooftops."

Consider these sentences:

"Drop the gun!" he roared threateningly.
"You can't make me," she snapped defiantly.
"Oh, please do that again," she gasped breathlessly.

None of those adverbs was necessary. Delete them and read the sentences again. See if you agree that they are actually stronger without those words. You might also want to avoid using words like "roared," "snapped," and "gasped," because they are words you might read in an old detective novel or romance magazine. "Said" works just fine most of the time and it doesn't get in the way of your story.

Qualifiers are words like *rather, quite, very,* and *little.* Try to avoid using too many of them. Examples of this are: *He was a rather quiet child. She was very embarrassed. They were a quite attentive group of students. I was a little afraid to read the letter.* All of those statements would be stronger without the qualifiers.

WHEN IN DOUBT, TAKE IT OUT!

One of the best secrets of good writing I ever learned was something I discovered by accident while I was editing a nonfiction book by a medical doctor. I kept coming across complicated sentences and couldn't figure out what the author meant. As he tried to explain them to me, I realized that he had already stated the ideas earlier in his manuscript and in a clearer way. In his efforts to reiterate what he thought was important, he had made his work more confusing. I found that it wasn't a matter of rewriting the lines to make them understandable. We could take the sentence out entirely without losing anything. His points then became more discernible and the writing flowed more gracefully.

You can't write clearly unless you are sure about what you want to say. I applied my new rule of "when in doubt, take it out" to other clients' works—as well as to my own—and the results were amazing.

Strip your writing of words and phrases that serve no function or are redundant. "The art of the writer," Ralph Waldo Emerson said, "is to speak his fact and have done. Let the reader find that he cannot afford to omit any line of your writing, because you have omitted every word that he can spare."

ACTIVE VERSUS PASSIVE VOICE

There are times to use the passive voice and times to use the active voice. But, generally, your writing will be more interesting if you use the active voice most of the time. Among the definitions of *passive* are:

submissive; not reacting visibly to something that might be expected to produce manifestations of an emotion or feeling . . . of, pertaining to, or being a voice, verb form, or construction having a subject represented as undergoing the action expressed by the verb, as the sentence *The letter was written last week.*

The definition of *active* is:

engaged in action or activity; characterized by energetic work, motion, etc. . . . of, pertaining to, or being a voice, verb form, or construction having a subject represented as performing or causing the action expressed by the verb, as the verb form *write* in *I write letters every day.*

SHOW, DON'T TELL

What exactly is meant by showing when we are only using words, not pictures? Telling is narrating what is happening. Showing is done through action and dialogue.

Telling is: *He was mean to the kid.*
Showing is: *He bopped the kid in the nose.*
Telling is: *She was being seductive.*
Showing is: *She said, "Darling, I have a present for you," as she slowly dropped the towel.*
Telling is: *He was bored.*
Showing is: *He looked at his watch and said, "How soon are we leaving?"*

We make our words come to life when we show rather than tell. Many writers also have a tendency to overexplain what is going on. A manuscript I recently edited made one area of showing, not telling, clear to me. The author frequently interrupted the narration to tell what the characters were thinking. He believed it was important to explain their motivations and feelings. However, it broke the momentum of the exciting story he had written and it distracted me so much that I took most of the "thinking" out, leaving in what they said and did.

When the author read my edited draft, he did not object to the cuts. As it was a mystery novel he was writing, getting rid of those digressions kept the story zipping along at a rapid pace and kept the reader involved. In this particular book, it wasn't important to know what the character was feeling. The author had defined the personalities of his characters very well as he introduced each one. After that it was, in fact, more interesting to speculate about the characters' thoughts and motivations.

A character can show what he is thinking by what he says and what he does. Using words to describe actions rather than thoughts usually works better. Showing can also be done through dialogue very effectively.

Instead of writing that John was startled when Marsha came up behind him, you could explain what your characters did.

Marsha crept up quietly behind John and whispered, "Well, hello, stranger!"

John jumped as though he had been struck. "Who the hell let you in here?" he said.

You could say that a character was angry or hurt or amused but it's more visual if you describe what a character did to show those feelings. Try to visualize your novel as a movie.

Showing is writing more externally, more expressively. Telling is usually more internal, giving an account of the action rather than describing the action in detail. Jim Lane, a writer friend of mine, said that he had been listening to an author interview on National Public Radio where the author asserted that "a novel is *all* telling—that is what a story is."

Jim made a good point when he said, "Usually we try to 'show' through dialogue because everything else is, by necessity, telling. Yet we would be hard-pressed to tell a story in dialogue alone. And sometimes telling—simple, declarative statements—is the most efficient way to advance the story."

It is certainly true that there are times when telling and using the passive voice move a story along best. Unless you are writing a script that will be interpreted by a director, you can't write only action and dialogue and maintain cohesiveness in a story.

As writers, we are faced with choices and decisions with every word we write. However, when presented with a choice, I always try action first, dialogue second, and everything else after that.

Similes, Metaphors, and Analogies

A simile is a figure of speech in which two unlike things are explicitly compared, as in, "O, my Luve is like a red, red rose," or, "the sun was like a luminescent orange," or, "the boy was sly as a fox."

A metaphor is a figure of speech in which a term or phrase is applied to something to which it is not literally applicable in order to suggest a resemblance, as in "A mighty fortress is our God" or "the autumn of her life." A critic once waxed metaphoric when he called James Michener "as sincere as his shoes." If you choose to use metaphors, please don't mix them up. In other words, don't start out by calling the sun an orange and end up calling it a volleyball.

An analogy is a similarity between like features of two things, a comparison. It is usually followed by *to, with,* or *between.* An example would be, "Do you really see a resemblance between our boss and Attila the Hun?"

We have all seen metaphors, similes, and analogies in novels, and when they are done well, they are delightful. They can add interest and make the narration more colorful. They should, however, be used sparingly or they will get in the way. Although they are useful devices, when you use too many of them they can become distracting. It's hard to tell a story well when you are concentrating more on clever expressions than on advancing the plot.

Clichés

A cliché is defined as a trite, stereotyped expression, such as *sadder but wiser, mad as a wet hen,* or *as strong as an ox.* It can also be a hackneyed plot, character development, use of form, or musical style. A cliché is anything that has become stale through overuse.

Lazy writers use clichés. Creative writers avoid them. If an expression comes easily, question it. In *A Dictionary of Modern English Usage* (1926), Francis George Fowler wrote that when hackneyed phrases come into the writer's mind they should be viewed as danger signals. "He should take warning that when they suggest themselves it is because what he is writing is bad stuff, or it would not need such help; let him see to the substance of his cake instead of decorating with sugarplums."

There was recently a politician who was so wont to use clichés that he was frequently quoted even though (or maybe because) there was very little substance in what he had to say. Here are a few that I found in one short speech he made:

"I think this thing is a *rush to judgment.*"
"We would not *sweep it under the rug.*"
"If you think you're going to win this on what public opinion polls say eighteen months out, *I beg to differ.*"
"He's going to be in for *a rude awakening.*"

Who is that cliché-addicted politician? No, it isn't George W. Bush, but as he might be one of your heroes, I'm not going to say. When it turned out the man was not going to run for president after all, the newspaper journalists were disappointed—he was such a rich source of trite expressions.

Although it is rare, occasionally there is a place for clichés. Vladimir Nabokov, in talking about his book *Lolita,* said, "In pornographic novels, action has to be limited to the copulation of clichés. Style, structure, imagery should never distract the reader from his tepid lust."

Sometimes clichés can be fun to use in dialogue. Many of them are colorful. Among my favorites are "nervous as a long-tailed cat in a room full of rocking chairs" and "busy as a one-armed paperhanger in a dust storm."

The caveat is: think carefully before you use a familiar phrase. Is there a reason for it? Does it fit so well that any other expression would not do? Does it define a character? If the answer to these questions is no, then try to express the same idea in an entirely new way.

SLANG AND JARGON

Unless it is dialogue peculiar to a character, or illustrates the era, or has a definite use in your particular work, do not use slang. Slang words and expressions are in a constant state of flux, slipping in and out of style in short spans of time. Therefore, using slang will date you or your book.

Hip, defined as "familiar with the latest ideas, styles, developments, etc.; up-to-date; with-it," was once *hep,* as in *hep cat.* These words probably originated with musicians.

Neat, cool, hot, bitchin', bad, righteous, fly, and *dope* are all words that mean very good-looking, exciting, sexy, or anything really terrific. *Phat,* a word that is used almost exclusively by teenagers, means roughly the same thing. Depending on which high-schooler I asked, I heard that it means pretty, hot and tempting, or something or someone extraordinarily appealing. *Extra large* means *really phat.*

A word that is acceptable in one culture may not be in another. Musicians may use one term while computer programmers use another to express the same idea. Slang will be different from one ethnic group and one region to another. Many of the slang expressions that have now become part of our language originated with avant-garde musicians of various eras, such as the pioneers of jazz, rock, and hip-hop. New language creators are often young people living in poor neighborhoods.

The use of profanity has changed, too. Swear words are used more widely than ever before by the general public. In many environments, such as the entertainment business, there are no longer any forbidden words. Anything goes. We hear a lot of swear words on the playground and in schools now, as children have incorporated them into their daily language. I don't wish to discuss the right or wrong of such a development but simply to call attention to the changing mores of language. But, morality aside, the overuse of profanity, like clichés, could show a lack of creativity.

While slang is associated with very informal idiomatic speech and is characterized by the use of vulgar vocabulary, jargon is often used by people in certain professions. Psychology has words that can't be found in most dictionaries. It is fine to use the jargon of your trade or profession when you are communicating with like-minded people, but it is not okay to use them in a book you want to reach a general readership.

Recently I've seen the use of such terms as "the F word" and "the N word" in written texts. I guess they are supposed to spare some imaginary person's delicate sensibilities, but we have all heard those words, including small children and great-grandmothers, so who are we protecting? Besides, words in and of themselves are not "bad." It is how they are used, who is saying them, and what is intended that can do harm. The word *nigger* in some contexts is not derogatory at all. Often black people call each other that as a term of endearment. It is when the word is used to disparage a person that it is wrong. When a word is used as a racial slur, or in any way that is hurtful, it is ugly. Even the so-called nice words like "honey" or "dear" can become very different words depending on the voice inflection and the way they are used. For example, "My dear, dear aunt died and the bitch left me absolutely nothing." Or a guy with a gun saying, "Give me all your money, honey, or I'll blow your head off."

I have no problem with the word *fuck* other than it is used so often and in so many different ways that it doesn't really serve to describe anything very well any more. I have been known to utter the word myself when I've been very upset, but I've never used it around my mother or my aunts or church people or school children. Not because I think it's a bad word but because they think it is and it would be offensive to them. I almost never use the word anymore because it is so overused that it has lost all of its impact. People who use *fuck* as an all-purpose word simply have no imagination.

When I was a little girl, my mother used to tell me, "Sticks and stones can break your bones but unkind words can't harm you." It's true that words are not things. If words were bullets, most of us would be dead. Words can hurt feelings, though, and they can kill love. So it's best to choose the words we use carefully and to be sensitive to the person who is listening to or reading them.

In a novel, the use of slang, profanity, jargon, and ethnic expressions can be instrumental in showing the identity or nature of a character. They can add color and authenticity. In nonfiction writing, however, unless the book is about slang or profanity, it's usually best to avoid them.

POINT OF VIEW

Should you write a novel in first person or third person? Many novels are written in first person as though the writer were writing about himself. In *Huckleberry Finn,* Mark Twain wrote in first person and in the dialect of a boy with a limited education. And he did it masterfully. Ernest Hemingway said that all modern American literature comes from that one book by Mark Twain. It might be tempting to try to follow his example but very few writers can do it well.

Writing in first person is usually hard for first-time novelists to do—and it is limiting. It gives you only one point of view, that of the protagonist. Most books are written in third person, the omniscient voice, because various points of view can be explored and it is easier to advance the story. Some authors go back and forth between first person and the omniscient voice. Some even mix several voices, each telling the story in first person. But these devices are hard to master and can be confusing and awkward. An author who does this very well is Barbara Kingsolver. She identifies whose point of view it is by using the character's name as the heading of the chapter.

Until you feel comfortable writing in first person or mixing up the voices and points of view of your characters, it might be better to stick to the omniscient voice.

PAST TENSE OR PRESENT TENSE

It is usually best to write in past tense, telling the story as though it has already happened. Writing in present tense often seems pretentious and unnatural. It also creates some problems when you try to tell the story "as it happens." You can't foreshadow events to come and you lack the perspective of looking back.

When you are writing a synopsis of your story, however, you should use the present tense. It gives it immediacy.

There are as many different ways to write as there are writers. Still, if you're going to do a thing, do it well. Don't take the easy way out. In his acceptance speech after he received the Nobel Prize, Ernest Hemingway said, "For a true writer each book should be a new beginning where he tries again for something that is beyond attainment."

Chapter 5

Plot, Story, and Characters

Writing a novel is like driving a car at night. You can see only as far as your headlights, but you can make the whole trip that way.

—E. L. DOCTOROW

A plot is a plan of action. Think of it as your chapter outline, where you show how your book opens, you list the major events, and you explain how the story ends. A theme is the central idea of a work. That would be your title and a brief sentence telling what the book is about. A story is the narration of events or series of events.

The story grows out of the characters, or it should. Even though it's always a good idea to have a plan to start out with, don't make the characters conform to it. Let the story serve the characters. Stephen King writes, "I distrust plot for two reasons: first, because our lives are largely plotless, even when you add in all our reasonable precautions and careful planning; and second, because I believe plotting and the spontaneity of real creation aren't compatible."

Although I would never disagree with such a master storyteller, I believe that you still have to know what kind of story you are telling, where you want to go with it, and what you hope to find at the end. It's comforting to have a map of some sort. Even if your plot is no better than a hand-drawn map to hidden treasure, and you find out the treasure isn't there, at least it is a guide. It's something to get you moving toward your goal. So I advise having a written plan and giving yourself the freedom to change it if your characters demand it.

You could think of your book as a jazz group where the story would be the song and the characters would be the musicians. All of the musicians are playing the same number in the same key and in basically the same time signature. They play together and listen to one another. But instead of playing every note that is written on the score, they improvise. They invent as they go along. Keeping the melody in their heads, they create a new way of interpreting the song. All truly great artists—whether musicians, novelists, painters, sculptors, or whatever—put their heart, their soul, their agonies, and their ecstasies into their work. It is more than an intellectual exercise for them. It is an exhilarating way of expressing their very essence—of revealing their deepest emotions.

As you tell your story, ask yourself constantly what each of your characters would do now. The plot will develop naturally and authentically as a result of the relationship between your characters. The story is what they do as opposed to what they should do. Their individual nature determines what happens. They influence each other's lives, just as jazz musicians influence each other's playing. You must know your characters, their mistakes in life, their addictions, neuroses, self-esteem or lack of it, what they love, who they love, and why. Your story sets up what is at stake for your major players and who is trying to take it away. You will establish the nature of the journey and what the destination is. Your characters will then decide which route they take, and what they do will determine whether they ever reach their goals. As the author, you choose the game—or song—your characters are playing and prepare a basic playing field on which they will perform. You can tell them the rules but your players will choose how or whether to play by them. Plot happens when a character is motivated to take some kind of action and another character or group of characters must respond to it. One incident leads to another, logically advancing the story.

Avoid excessive exposition. Do not give any exposition before the story begins. Let the exposition come through what your characters say and do. Although flashbacks are generally frowned upon by book publishers (and by television and film directors, too) they can be a useful tool in giving the reader some back story. Flashbacks can help explain the character's emotional state. This can be done through what a character recalls of past events, either through what she says or what she thinks. As tempting as it is to use flashbacks to fill in some blanks, please use them sparingly. They interrupt the story.

As the omniscient storyteller, do as little explaining as possible. Let your characters handle that task through dialogue. Stay in the active voice most of the time, using the passive voice when it is more appropriate for moving the story along.

Before you begin writing your book, write what you know or think you know about each of your major characters. Know your protagonist (the main character, usually the hero) and your antagonist (a major character opposing the protagonist) well. What are they looking for? What or who is standing in the way of their getting it? What was their childhood like? How are they different from each other? What are their personalities like? Arrogant? Shy? Self-centered? Religious or sacrilegious? Noble or ignominious? Beware of making your protagonist too good or your antagonist too bad. Nothing is more boring than a gorgeous, saintly human being who never makes a mistake or says an unkind word. No reader will be able to identify with a person like that. Also be careful not to make your antagonist pure evil with no redeeming virtues. It is much more interesting to show a vicious hit man, for example, who never misses Sunday mass, or who lovingly coaches his daughter's basketball team.

When you start writing your book, introduce and describe your protagonist early on. With each new character who enters your story, especially if he is to play a major role, tell the reader something about him. The following are excerpts from books where the author did this very well.

CHARACTER DESCRIPTIONS

Mr. Bennet was so odd a mixture of quick parts, sarcastic humour, reserve, and caprice, that the experience of three and twenty years had been insufficient to make his wife understand his character. *Her* [Mrs. Bennet's] mind was less difficult to develop. She was a woman of mean understanding, little information, and uncertain temper. When she was discontented she fancied herself nervous. The business of her life was to get her daughters married; its solace was visiting and news.

—FROM *PRIDE AND PREJUDICE* BY JANE AUSTIN

Kate Blackwell was a slim, petite woman, with a regal bearing that made her appear taller than she was. She had a face that one remembered. A proud bone structure, dawn-gray eyes and a stubborn chin, a blending of her Scottish and Dutch ancestors. She had fine, white hair that once had been a luxuriant black cascade, and against the graceful folds of her ivory velvet dress, her skin had the soft translucence old age sometimes brings.

—FROM *MASTER OF THE GAME* BY SIDNEY SHELDON

He was most fifty, and he looked it. His hair was long and tangled and greasy, and hung down, and you could see his eyes shining through like he was behind vines. It was all black, no gray; so was his long mixed-up whiskers. There warn't no color in his face, where his face showed; it was white; not like another man's white, but a white to make a body sick, a white to make a body's flesh crawl—a tree-toad white, a fishbelly white. As for his clothes—just rags, that was all. He had one ankle resting on t'other knee; the boot on that foot was busted, and two of his toes stuck through, and he worked them now and then.

—FROM *HUCKLEBERRY FINN* BY MARK TWAIN

Winterbourne looked along the path and saw a beautiful young lady advancing. . . . She was dressed in white muslin, with a hundred frills and flounces, and knots of pale-coloured ribbon. [Her] glance was perfectly direct and unshrinking . . . her eyes were singularly honest and fresh. They were wonderfully pretty eyes; and, indeed, Winterbourne had not seen for a long time anything prettier than his fair countrywoman's various features—her complexion, her nose, her ears, her teeth. [Her face] was not at all insipid, but it was not exactly expressive.

—FROM *DAISY MILLER: A STUDY* BY HENRY JAMES

Margie Young-Hunt came in, pert-breasted in a salmon sweater. Her tweed skirt clung lovingly in against her thighs and tucked up under her proud fanny, but it was in her eyes, her brown myopic eyes, that Ethan saw what his wife could never see because it wasn't there when wives were about. This was a predator, a huntress, Artemis for pants. Old Cap'n Hawley called it a "roving eye." It was in her voice too, a velvet growl that changed to a thin, mellow confidence for wives.

—FROM *THE WINTER OF OUR DISCONTENT* BY JOHN STEINBECK

From the age of twelve Kay Tompkins had worn men like rings on every finger. Her face was round, young, pretty and strong; a strength accentuated by the responsive play of brows and lashes around her clear, glossy hazel eyes. . . . There was that excitement about her that seemed to reflect the excitement of the world.

—FROM THE SHORT STORY "MAGNETISM" BY F. SCOTT FITZGERALD

Good character descriptions aren't just about what the person looks like; they contain germs of personality, nuances of motivations, and foreshadowings of later events. In the first example, Jane Austen is more interested in describing the personalities of Mr. and Mrs. Bennet than in what they look like. You get a hint at what is to come when you learn that "the business of her [Mrs. Bennet's] life was to get her daughters married." Therein lies the seed of the story.

Sidney Sheldon describes his protagonist's physical appearance and, although he doesn't say it directly, you get a sense of her strong personality and the fact that she is wealthy.

Mark Twain, genius that he was, paints a vivid word portrait of Huck's father. He gives details about his physical appearance that tell you his age, that he is poor, unkempt, dirty, and probably drunk. You get a feeling there is something very ominous about the man and that he is going to figure in the story later on.

Steinbeck's description of Margie Young-Hunt, "pert-breasted," and with a "proud fanny" foreshadows her goal of seducing the protagonist, Ethan Hawley. Fitzgerald describes a similar type of woman in Kay Tompkins who "had worn men like rings on every finger." You know in each case that those women are going to cause someone a lot of grief.

PACE AND DYNAMICS

Make sure your story is like life with its ups and downs. It should be dynamic, marked by continuous change, activity, or progress. Some of your days should be calm, warm, and sunny and others cold, gray, and rainy. You need full-moon nights and sun-darkening storms. You need drama, certainly, but you need quiet moments, too.

Your story should have a climax and a few turning points of varying degrees. A climax is the point of high emotional intensity at which a story reaches its peak. You also need to pace your story. There need to be moments where the pace is slow as your characters are engaged in introspection or in getting to know each other. As the story progresses, quicken the pace. Accelerate the action as you approach climactic points, making your sentences simpler and shorter, easier to read and understand. Imagine a friendship turning into a torrid romance and culminating in making love. Think of a symphony orchestra playing Ravel's *Bolero*. If the whole piece were played at one level of volume, with no dynamics or change of pace, it would become dull and meaningless.

Anne Lamott, who also sees the analogy of writing to music, explains the climax as "that one major event, usually toward the end, that brings all the tunes you have been playing so far into one major chord, after which at least one of your players is profoundly changed." If your protagonist has not changed in a major way from the beginning to the end of your book, you have no story.

And at the end, who won? Who lost? What is the payoff? What is the grand finale? You may not know the answers now. You might not find out until your entire book has been written and all the characters have played their roles. And maybe that's as it should be.

Chapter 6

Writing Nonfiction

Ah yet, ere I descend to the grave
May I a small house and large garden have;
And a few friends, and many books, both true,
Both wise, and both delightful too!

—ABRAHAM COWLEY

There's no reason for nonfiction to be any less delightful than fiction. A good storyteller can make trigonometry exciting. Thus, many of the points made in the previous chapter apply to nonfiction as well as to novels.

Nonfiction is the broadest category of written works. There are different ways you would write in each genre. Histories and biographies focus on stories; cookbooks contain mostly lists; how-to books explain processes and procedures.

Accuracy is essential in nonfiction. And, in my opinion, so is truth. I have known writers who want to make a true story more exciting by inventing incidents that never happened. I choose not to cross that line between fact and fiction. Sometimes you may have to bend time and place a little to shorten what might be an overlong or tedious story, but I believe that, too, should be avoided whenever possible. Changing the time or place of an event should never be done when writing a history.

Webster's New Universal Unabridged Dictionary defines non-fiction as "the branch of literature comprising works of narrative prose dealing with or offering opinions or conjectures upon facts and reality, including biography, history, and the essay (opposed to *fiction* and distinguished from *poetry* and *drama*)." Under its listing for fiction it states, "Fiction suggests a story invented and fashioned either to entertain or to deceive." Nonfiction should not deceive but it certainly can and, whenever possible and appropriate, *should* entertain.

How do you make a nonfiction book entertaining? You avoid stilted language, for starters. If your book is for a general readership, you will want to avoid using words that are not familiar to your average reader. You follow the same rules of good composition that you would if you were writing a novel. That includes avoiding long complicated sentences, repetitions, and redundancies.

INTERVIEWING

If you were writing a contemporary biography or a true crime book, you probably would have to interview quite a few people. It can sometimes be difficult to get at the truth, because different people will recall the same event differently. Just ask any police detective how accurate eyewitnesses are and how many of them agree on exactly what happened. That is why circumstantial evidence is often more dependable than the testimony of witnesses. How can you know who to believe? You can't. You can only interview as many knowledgeable people as possible, ask very specific questions, and record the answers you get. You must do as much fact-checking as you can. Then you have to make some tough decisions as to what to write and how to write it.

I have been both an interviewer and an interviewee. I am always a little tense when I am being interviewed, because very often the interviewer does not get the facts straight or reports what I have told her in confidence. It is now embedded in my brain: *never tell a reporter anything you don't want reported.* Only rarely have interviewers sent me their copy before it was published. But I think that is the courteous thing to do and I nearly always do that when

I interview anyone. I try to record (with their permission) my interviews, because when I try to write fast I can't read it later. That way you don't have to rely on your undecipherable notes or your memory.

If you are writing a biography, how do you get people to tell you the interesting stuff? Here is an interview trick I learned by accident when I worked as researcher and writer for the TV show *This Is Your Life* in the mid-1980s. I had to interview the people who were acquainted with the person whose life story we were going to tell on the show. When I asked questions of the subject's family, friends, teachers, and so forth, they always wanted to portray the subject in the best light possible. "He was always so polite." "She always acted like such a perfect little lady." Well, we all know that a person who never makes mistakes or does anything wrong makes for a drab, uninteresting story. I certainly wasn't trying to get any dirt on the subject, a noted scientist in this case, because the show was about celebrating a life, not trashing it. However, I wanted some interesting, funny, or unusual stories about the man. The TV show was designed to entertain, after all!

Most of the interviews were conducted on the phone. There were the usual questions I had to ask. Where was he born? What was he like as a child? How many children in the family? What were his interests, hobbies? You know, all the basic information. Once I had the facts, I concentrated on what made this person different from everyone else. When I spoke with his siblings, I asked things like What kind of brother was he? Did he tease you? What incidents from your childhood stand out? One day when I couldn't seem to get the subject's sister to tell me anything interesting about the man whose story we wanted to do, I sat silent for a long time trying to think of what more to ask. The woman on the other end of the line finally could stand the silence no longer. "Hello, are you still there?" she asked. I replied yes and then she proceeded to tell me the most amazing story about her brother. She had been reluctant to talk about the event, because Bob had ditched school that day, something he did often but was able to keep from his mother, an overworked single parent. One day Bob and another boy had gone fishing in the river when they heard someone call for help. Forgetting that he had never learned to swim, Bob managed to get to the little girl who was choking and thrashing about in the middle of the river. His friend tied a small tree branch to the end of a rope and threw it out to Bob. Bob was able to grab it with one hand while holding the struggling child's head above water with the other. Bob's friend then pulled Bob and the little girl in to shore. Bob and the child were lying on the ground gasping for air when the girl's mother ran over, picked her up, and rushed her to the hospital. The child's mother later tried to find the boy who had rescued her child to thank him but Bob didn't want to be found because he knew he'd get into trouble for skipping school. No one but Bob's friend and sister ever knew he had saved a child's life at great risk to his own, and he made them both promise never to tell.

With Bob's sister's help we were able to track down the girl, now grown and with a family of her own. The host of the show told the story, then paused, and a voice offstage said, "Bob, I never saw you again since then, but I want to thank you now." The girl walked onstage crying and laughing at the same time, then rushed into Bob's arms. That was the highlight of the show.

From then on I knew what to do when an interviewee was reticent. I simply stopped talking and waited. It always worked. That's when I got my best material.

ORGANIZING YOUR MATERIAL

If you haven't done so already, put your written interviews, your research notes, and all other material you have gathered in separate folders. Then begin putting the book together. This is where doing a book proposal first will be helpful. You will already have done a chapter-by-chapter outline and decided what your chapters will contain. If you haven't done that yet, that is your next step. Then, start writing. At this point don't be concerned with the art of writing; just get it all down on paper. You can go back later to embellish and fine-tune it.

Chapter 7

Editing Principles

I can't write five words but that I change seven.

—DOROTHY PARKER

With computers, more writers are able to produce works on their own. They don't have to hire someone to type their manuscripts for them. They can edit, rewrite, and make changes easily and quickly on the computer. That means publishers are getting an avalanche of manuscripts. With competition stiffer and book publishers' profit margins smaller than ever, books needing extensive editing are often rejected. As many publishers don't have the staff they once had, their decision about whether to publish your book may depend on how much work needs to be done on it. When they find a book they like that has also been well edited, they are more likely to take it on.

Many writers are now hiring professional editors to put the final polish on their manuscripts before they send them off. But that can be costly, so it's best to edit as much as you can first. In addition to the obvious—incorrect spelling and grammar—here are some other things to look out for.

- Words repeated in a sentence
- Repetitions of all kinds: phrases, ideas, descriptions
- Long, complex sentences
- A string of choppy sentences

- Inconsistencies in style and punctuation
- Inconsistencies in tense (past, present, future)

STYLEBOOKS

If you have no other reference books, it is essential that you have an up-to-date dictionary and a stylebook and refer to them often. *The Elements of Style* is probably the most user-friendly of them all. It covers elementary rules of usage, principles of composition, form, and writing styles. It's a small book—the edition I have contains only 105 pages, including the index—but there is an amazing amount of information and wisdom stuffed into this classic. *The Elements of Style* has been around for nearly a century but it is timeless. Even though it has been revised and reprinted many times, the basic information has not changed greatly since the first edition. My issue was copyrighted in 2000.

Another stylebook is *The Associated Press Stylebook and Libel Manual*. This book is mainly for journalists but it would be helpful to any writer. It contains over five thousand entries explaining the AP's rules on grammar, spelling, punctuation, and usage. An added plus is that it includes advice on how writers can avoid libel and copyright infringement. The *AP Stylebook* is organized like a dictionary and it, too, is user-friendly.

Most book publishers use and recommend *The Chicago Manual of Style*. It is the most comprehensive of them all and the most difficult to use. The first edition of this reference book was published in 1906. I have an edition that was published in 1993 and, at 921 pages, it is almost 200 pages longer than the previous 1982 issue. With a cover price of $40, it is not an inexpensive book. But it is worth every bit of the cost.

The *Manual* is considered by many to be essential for all writers, editors, proofreaders, copywriters, publishers, and anyone else who works with words. Although the publisher states that it's easier to use than ever before, it still takes some getting used to. Even though I use it frequently in my work, I find it hard to locate quickly just what I'm looking for. It can be frustrating until you become familiar with the way the book is laid out. The *Manual* contains a wealth of information on many subjects. In addition to word usage, abbreviations, titles, forms of address, punctuation, and all of those details, it also covers manuscript preparation, rights, and permissions and many other subjects. Manners of writing and word usage change constantly, so it's best to get the latest issue.

STYLES CHANGE

Since the advent of the computer, some typing styles have changed. One example is that instead of spacing twice after a period and before the next sentence, as we did when we typed on a typewriter, we now space only once. When we used a typewriter, there were no italics available, so we underlined book titles. On a computer we can italicize them. On the typewriter we used the carriage return at the end of each line, but on the computer we use word wrap. The word-processing program allows us to go to the next line automatically. It can even hyphenate words automatically when we select that feature.

I will cover some of the more common questions I get from writers regarding styles, but it's not possible to address all the things that have changed in this book. When you have any doubts at all about styles, refer to a good stylebook.

DICTIONARIES

Always, always, always use a dictionary when you have any questions at all about the spelling or the meaning of a word. Many of us misspell or use words inaccurately without realizing it and the wrong word can change the meaning of a sentence drastically. Spell-check on the computer is helpful but it doesn't contain as many words as a good desk dictionary. And it doesn't catch a word that is spelled right but used wrong.

For spelling, the *Chicago Manual of Style* recommends *Webster's Third New International Dictionary* and its abridged *Merriam Webster's Collegiate Dictionary. Webster's New Universal Unabridged Dictionary* (based on the Second Edition of the *Random House Dictionary of the English Language*) is also considered outstanding. *Washington Post Book World* calls it "without a doubt, today's unabridged dictionary of choice."

For more casual use, there is the *Random House Webster's College Dictionary* and Houghton Mifflin's *Webster's II: New College Dictionary*, which I think I like better of the two. Unlike the unabridged, these are small enough to fit on a desk. Whichever dictionary you choose, use the same one throughout the editing of each manuscript so that you will be consistent. When two spellings of a word are given, use the first listed because it is the preferred spelling.

ACCURACY

Leave nothing to chance. Check everything you have any doubts about. Is it one word, a hyphenated word, or two words? For instance, you would write "this is for your *eyes only*" but "this is an *eyes-only* report." Both *crow's-nest* and *crow's nest* are acceptable, depending on the usage, but *crowsnest* is not a word. Different dictionaries may have different spellings for the same word. Sometimes it takes a few years for a new word to settle down to one preferred spelling. Some words never seem to, such as *e-mail*. Some dictionaries show three spellings of it: E-mail, e-mail, and email. Others show only one or two. So make a choice and use it consistently.

There are words that you may not find in any dictionary that's less than five or ten years old. If you can't find a dictionary that contains newly coined words, check several sources, such as newspapers, magazines, and computer manuals for these words. But even that may not help you. I've seen *Web site* spelled *web site*, and *website*, although it appears that most authorities have now settled on *Web site*. When in doubt, choose one and stick to it throughout your manuscript. The main thing, again, is to be consistent.

Your computer's spell-check is helpful but has its limitations. Beware of errors it will not pick up, such as using *their* (possessive case of *they*) when it should be *there* (in or at that place) and *emigrate* (to leave a country to live elsewhere) when you mean *immigrate* (to enter a country to live there).

Here is a list of words that are frequently confused and misused. Some sound a little alike and a few sound exactly alike, which is one of the reasons they are misused. And we can't depend on our computer's spell-check. Among the errors it will not pick up are words that are spelled correctly but are used incorrectly.

absorb	take in; reduce the effect of; deal easily with; consume
adsorb	to gather a substance on a surface in a dissolved layer (chemistry)
accept	receive; answer affirmatively
except	leave out, exclude
acclamation	an expression of enthusiastic approval
acclimation	adaptation of an organism to its natural climatic environment
adapt	fit; adjust; alter or modify
adept	thoroughly proficient; an expert
adopt	take another's child as one's own; choose to follow; accept
adverse	unfavorable
averse	reluctant; opposed
advice	an opinion or recommendation
advise	give counsel to
affect	to influence: *The plan will affect the outcome.*
effect	a result; an influence: *His protest had no effect.*
aid	to help or assist
aide	an assistant
alley	narrow back street
ally	confederate
all ready	completely ready
already	previously; so soon
allusion	an indirect reference
illusion	an unreal or false impression
altar	a table or platform used in a church service
alter	to change

amend	make minor improvements; correct an error
emend	edit a text to remove errors and corruptions
ante-	before
anti-	against
appraise	determine the worth of
apprise	give notice of; inform; acquaint
ascent	the act or process of moving upward
assent	agreement as to a plan or proposal; consent
auger	a tool
augur	a prophet (noun); to prophesy (verb)
bail	money in exchange for release of a prisoner; remove water from a boat
bale	a large, bound package of material
baited	lured; enticed; placed bait on a hook
bated	lessened the force of; moderated: *with bated breath and whispering*
bazaar	a shop; a fair where merchandise is sold
bizarre	strikingly unconventional or far-fetched
beside	at the side of
besides	in addition to
bight	middle part of a rope; bend in the shore; bay or gulf
bite	cut or wound with the teeth
byte	adjacent bits processed by a computer as a unit
bloc	coalition of groups or nations with the same purpose
block	solid piece of hard material such as wood or stone; an obstruction
blond	light-colored hair or complexion; a person with fair hair or skin
blonde	a blond-haired woman
born	brought forth by birth
borne	past participle of the verb bear: to support

bough	tree branch
bow	to bend or yield
brake	reduce speed; a retarding device
break	separate; destroy; fracture
breach	a violation, as of a law, obligation, or promise
breech	the lower rear portion of a human trunk; buttocks
buy	purchase
by	next to, close to
bye	a secondary matter; a side issue; incidentally: *bye the by*
bye-bye	var. of good-bye; used to express farewell
cache	a hiding place; a hidden store of goods
cash	currency or coins
callous	unfeeling, hard, indifferent, unsympathetic
callus	a hardened or thickened part of the skin
Calvary	site of Jesus' crucifixion
cavalry	mounted soldiers
cannon	a mounted gun
canon	ecclesiastical rule or law; a standard, criterion
canvas	closely woven, heavy cloth; a painting on canvas
canvass	to examine or seek opinions; analyze; explore
capital	money; a seat of government
capitol	legislature building
carat	the weight of precious stones, especially diamonds
caret	a writer's and proofreader's mark
karat	the proportion of pure gold used with an alloy
caregiver	a person who cares for someone sick or disabled
caretaker	a person in charge of maintenance of a building or estate
caster	a roller
castor	a bean and the oil derived from it
censer	a container in which incense is burned
censor	prohibit or restrict the use of something
censure	criticize harshly; reprove; condemn

cession	act of ceding
session	meeting
chafe	to rub
chaff	worthless matter
chord	musical tones
cord	thin rope
cite	to quote; refer to as an example; to commend
sight	vision; a view; mental perception
site	position; location; place
clamber	to climb with hands and feet; a difficult climb
clamor	loud shouting or noise; a protest; an appeal or demand
climactic	pertaining to or coming to a climax
climacteric	a period of decrease of reproductive capacity; any critical period
climatic	of or pertaining to climate
compare	to liken; relate; examine similarities
contrast	examine differences
complacent	self-satisfied; calmly content
complaisant	eager to please; deferential
complement	something that completes
compliment	an expression of admiration; praise
compose	create or put together
comprise	to contain; to include all
confidant	a friend to whom secrets are confided (fem. *confidante*)
confident	having strong belief; sure; certain; self-assured
conscience	faculty for recognizing the difference between right and wrong
conscious	aware; capable of thought, will, or perception
consul	diplomat
council	assembly
counsel	advice; a lawyer

continual	intermittent; often repeated
continuous	uninterrupted in time
corporal	of the body
corporeal	material, tangible
councilor	member of a council
counselor	one who gives advice
credible	believable or worthy of belief
creditable	bringing credit or honor
criminalist	a forensic investigator
criminologist	one who studies crime
cue	a reminder; prompting; hint
queue	a waiting line of people or cars; a pigtail
deduce	infer; draw as a logical conclusion
deduct	subtract; take away from
defuse	to remove the fuse; to make less dangerous
diffuse	to pour out and spread; widely scattered
demur	take exception; object
demure	shy; modest; reserved; retiring
deprecate	express disapproval of; deplore
depreciate	diminish in value; disparage; belittle
desert	a dry, barren region; something deserved; to forsake, abandon
dessert	a usually sweet food served as the last course of a meal
dialectal	of a dialect
dialectic	of logical argumentation
disassemble	take to pieces
dissemble	talk or act hypocritically; disguise or conceal
disburse	pay out; spend
disperse	scatter; dissipate; spray
discomfit	to confuse, frustrate
discomfort	to make uncomfortable

discreet	circumspect, prudent
discrete	separate
dual	for two, double
duel	fight
elicit	to draw or bring out; educe; evoke
illicit	not legally permitted; unlicensed; unlawful
emigrate	to leave a country to live elsewhere
immigrate	to enter a country to live there
emanant	issuing from a source
eminent	prominent; outstanding; distinguished; noteworthy
immanent	existing or remaining within; inherent; subjective
imminent	about to occur at any moment; impending
energize	give energy to
enervate	destroy the vigor of; weaken
ensure	guarantee
insure	protect against loss
equable	uniform
equitable	fair, just
exacerbate	intensify, inflame, worsen
exasperate	incense, anger, vex, irritate
exercise	physical, mental, or spiritual activity
exorcise	expel a supposed evil spirit from a person or place
farther	at or to a greater distance, degree, or extent
further	same as above; also means "moreover" and "additional"
ferment	agitation; unrest; excitement; organism that causes fermentation
foment	incite; provoke; inflame; instigate discord or rebellion
flair	skill, talent; aptitude
flare	a bright light, an outburst
flammable	combustible (technical use: often seen on a warning sign)
inflammable	combustible (often used figuratively: inflammable emotions)

flaunt	show off; display ostentatiously
flout	show contempt for; scoff at
flounder	move clumsily or jerkily; flop about
founder	bog down or become disabled
forbear	to refrain or abstain from; to forgo
forebear	ancestor; forefather; progenitor
forceful	powerful
forcible	done by force
forego	go before; to precede
forgo	give up; renounce
foreword	introduction in a book; a preface
forward	toward or to what is in front of
fort	a fortified place occupied by troops; an army post
forte	an activity in which one excels; in music: loudly, forcefully
fortuitous	happening by chance
fortunate	lucky
gaff	a metal hook fastened to a pole
gaffe	a faux pas
gage	a security or a pledge
gauge	a measuring device; the size of shotguns
gamble	to bet
gambol	to frolic
gamut	the whole series or range or scope of anything
gantlet	an ordeal, an attack from all sides (also *gauntlet*)
gauntlet	a glove; a challenge: *take up the gauntlet*
gibe	jeer or taunt
jibe	be in agreement or shift sails
gorilla	an ape
guerrilla	a member of a military force
gourmand	a person who likes food and tends to eat to excess
gourmet	a connoisseur of fine food and drink

grisly	gruesome
grizzly	grayish or flecked with gray; a grizzly bear
hail	acclaim; attract: *hail a cab*
hale	healthy, robust, vigorous
hangar	shed for airplanes
hanger	frame for hanging clothes
hoard	a stash (noun); to store away (verb)
horde	a wandering group or a swarm
hurdle	a barrier over which contestants must leap; problem; obstacle
hurtle	speed, race, rush, shoot
hyper-	excessive, above
hypo-	insufficient, under
idle	not in use; unemployed; inactive
idol	an object of worship; a false god; a person or thing blindly adored
idyll	a scene of rural simplicity; a narrative poem; carefree experience
illegible	impossible or hard to read
unreadable	not interesting; not worth reading
imply	indicate
infer	draw a conclusion
incredible	unbelievable
incredulous	skeptical
indiscreet	lacking prudence; revealing secrets
indiscrete	not divided into distinct parts
ingenious	brilliant, clever
ingenuous	simple, naive
inter-	between, among
intra-	within
its	belonging to it
it's	it is

lay	set down; place or put; past tense of *lie*
lie	rest in a horizontal position; recline
lead	to conduct, guide, or escort; a heavy bluish-gray metal
led	past tense of lead: *He led them along the path.*
lessen	to cause to decrease; to belittle; to become less
lesson	something to be learned; a class; a teaching
loath	unwilling, reluctant, disinclined: *She was loath to go.*
loathe	to detest, abominate, hate: *They loathe each other.*
liable	responsible; likely: *She's liable to bring a date.*
libel	a defamatory statement
loose	not tight or bound; to make loose
lose	to experience loss
luxuriant	abundant, lush
luxurious	sumptuous
magnate	a person of great influence
magnet	a thing or person that attracts
main	chief; principal
mane	long hair on the neck of a horse, lion, etc.; a person's long hair
manner	a way of doing something; one's bearing or behavior
manor	a landed estate; mansion
mantel	facing of a fireplace; a shelf above
mantle	a cloak; something that conceals
mall	a large retail complex; a large area used as a public walk
maul	a heavy hammer or club; to use roughly; to injure
mean	intermediate value of number sequence
mien	a person's look or bearing; demeanor
median	middle number in number sequence
miner	one who mines
minor	underage person
missal	a book of prayers or devotions
missile	an object or weapon for throwing or shooting

moral	ethical; lesson
morale	spirit, mood
naval	of the navy
navel	umbilicus
notable	worthy, impressive
notorious	widely known and ill-regarded, as a notorious criminal
ordinance	law; practice or custom; religious rite
ordnance	military weapons as a whole; heavy guns; artillery
palate	the roof of the mouth; taste
palette	an artist's paint board
pallet	bed, platform
peace	calmness; lack of hostility
piece	a part
peak	pinnacle, acme, zenith
peek	to look or glance quickly or furtively
pique	offend, sting, irritate, affront
pedal	a foot-operated lever
peddle	to carry from place to place to sell; to deal out or distribute
persecute	hound, afflict, torture, torment
prosecute	to institute legal proceedings against
perspective	vision, view
prospective	future; potential or expected
plain	simple; clear; frank
plane	airplane; to smooth
poor	needy, penniless, destitute, poverty-stricken
pore	to read with steady attention; a minute orifice as in the skin
pour	to send a liquid flowing or falling; to rain heavily
practicable	feasible
practical	suited to actual conditions; sensible
precede	to go before
proceed	to continue

prescribe	appoint; to order a medicine
proscribe	prohibit; banish or exile
principal	main, foremost; the person in charge
principle	a moral rule; a law
prophecy	a prediction of future events (noun)
prophesy	to speak as a prophet; to foretell future events (verb)
prostate	gland
prostrate	lying flat
quiet	still
quite	very
rack	framework; spread out; torture
wrack	damage or destruction
ravage	wreak great destruction or devastation
ravish	abduct, rape, or carry away with emotion
rebuff	a rejection; a repulse; a snub (noun); reject (verb)
rebuke	reprove sharply (verb); the act of rebuking (noun); a reproof
rebut	to argue to the contrary
regime	a system of government; a mode of rule
regimen	a regulated course, as of diet or exercise
regiment	a military unit of ground forces
rain	shower; to send or pour down
reign	the period a ruler is on the throne
rein	the leather strap for controlling a horse
reluctant	disinclined; unwilling to act
reticent	unwilling to speak
retch	to make efforts to vomit
wretch	an unfortunate or unhappy person
right	correct; proper; just; appropriate
rite	religious ceremony; a ceremonial act
role	a part played by an actor; position; duty
roll	to turn; a small bread

seasonable	appropriate to the season; timely
seasonal	depending on the season
shear	to cut or clip
sheer	transparent; utter
stair	a step or a flight of steps
stare	a steady gaze; to look at intently
stationary	fixed; not migratory
stationery	paper supplies
stanch	to stop the flow of blood or other liquid
staunch	constant, true, faithful, steadfast: *He is a staunch conservative.*
taught	past tense of teach: *He taught me to sing.*
taut	trim; tidy; neat; tightly drawn; tense: *She speaks in short, taut sentences.*
temblor	a tremor; earthquake
trembler	a person or thing that trembles
than	used after comparative words such as other (conjunction)
then	at that time; immediately or soon afterward; next in order
their	possessive case of they
there	in or at that place
they're	they are
throe	upheaval, tumult, chaos, turmoil
throw	fling, launch, send
to	toward
too	also; excessive
two	number
tortuous	full of twists, turns, or bends; circuitous; devious
torturous	pertaining to torture or suffering: *They toil in the torturous heat.*
trooper	soldier or police officer
trouper	actor; dependable person
trustee	a person to whom is given the control of another's property
trusty	a prisoner given special privileges for good behavior

vain	egotistical, proud, arrogant; fruitless; trivial
vane	a blade in a wheel to be moved by air, steam, or water
vein	blood vessel; a natural channel; tone; touch; thread
venal	corrupt
venial	pardonable
verses	stanzas; poems or pieces of poetry
versus	against; as compared to; in contrast with
whose	possessive case of which or who
who's	who is
wreak	inflict punishment; express anger; vent
wreck	destroy; tear down; the remains of something ruined
reek	to give off a strong odor
wright	one who constructs something; playwright
write	form letters on a surface; compose; screenwriter
your	belonging to you
you're	you are

Also be careful in using qualifying or quantifying adjectives or adverbs with words that are absolutes. An example of this kind of misuse that is frequently seen is *very unique*. *Unique* is an absolute, like *perfect, complete, equal, demolish, destroy, dead,* and *pregnant*. *Unique* means existing as the only one or as the sole example. *Perfect* describes an absolute condition that cannot exist in degrees. *Demolish* and *destroy* mean to end the existence of. It would be redundant to say *totally demolished* or *completely destroyed*. And we all know that you can't be *a little pregnant* or *a little dead*. There can't be a little or a lot of an absolute. It either is or it isn't; you either are or you aren't.

Other words frequently misused are "that" when it should be "who" as in "Is she the woman *that* sold you the hat?" instead of "Is she the woman *who* sold you the hat?" A person is a *who*. A thing is a *that*.

Was is sometimes used in the subjunctive mood when the appropriate word is *were*. Subjunctive is a grammatical mood typically used for doubtful or hypothetical statements. For example, one would say *when I was young* but *if I were young.*

The word "whom" has gone almost completely out of style. And good riddance. Most people use it incorrectly anyway. The following is from *Random House Webster's College Dictionary:*

> By the strict rules of grammar, "who" is the correct form for the subject of a sentence or clause (*Who said that? The guard who let us in checked our badges*), and "whom" is used for the object of a verb or preposition (*Whom did you ask? To whom are we obliged for this assistance?*). These distinctions are observed less and less in current English. The usage cited above is characteristic of formal editing and is generally followed in edited prose. In natural informal speech, however, "whom" is quite rare. "Whom" still prevails as the object of a preposition when the preposition immediately precedes (*all patients with whom you have had contact*), but this juxtaposition tends to be avoided in both speech and writing, esp. in questions (*Who is this gift from?*) and sometimes by omission of the pronoun altogether (*all patients you have had contact with*).

REDUNDANCIES

It seems that so much writing is rife with redundancies these days. The most common one I see is "reason why." Say "It is the *reason* I told you that" or "It is *why* I told you that" instead of "It is the *reason why* I told you that." You don't need both words.

Avoid tautologizing as much as you can. Tautology is the needless repetition of an idea in different words, as in "widow woman." Good writing is taut (tidy, neat, trim), not tautologous.

Here's a list of redundancies that appear often, not only in everyday conversation and in writers' manuscripts, but in newspapers, magazines, and even on television newscasts.

absolutely certain	actual fact
added bonus	just exactly
radiate out	raise up

revert back
resume again
right-hand side
alternative choice
meet together
same identical
and also
sum total
drop down
enter into
protrude out
forward progress
annual birthday
cash money

regular routine
reiterate again
left-hand side
may possibly be
minute detail
separate out
completely full
deadly killer
fatal suicide
time when
previous history
baby kitten
follow behind

OMIT WORDS YOU DON'T NEED

To quote *The Elements of Style,* "A sentence should contain no unnecessary words, a paragraph no unnecessary sentences, for the same reason that a drawing should have no unnecessary lines and a machine no unnecessary parts." Instead of saying *due to the fact that,* you could just say *because.* Instead of *in order to,* simply say *to.*

CONSISTENCY

Check for tense. If you are writing in present tense, be sure that you don't slip into past tense.

Once you decide on a *style,* stick with it. Style is defined as the rules of uniformity in punctuation, capitalization, spelling, word division, and other details of expression. They often vary according to custom. Textbook publishers require a different style than publishers of romance novels, for example. Knowing the styles they use and abiding by them will make you appear more experienced in that field of writing.

When you are writing nonfiction, don't move back and forth between formal and informal speech. The voice of your characters should also be consistent. If you are writing a novel and you give your character a certain pattern of speech, stay with it throughout the book. If he would normally say "I ain't done nothin'," don't have him sometimes say "I haven't done anything."

REPETITION

Once you have stated a character's title, described how she looks or what he does, don't do it again unless you have a good reason. If you feel that it's important to remind the reader who this person is, say it differently, put a new twist on it.

Some writers have a tendency to begin a lot of sentences with the same phrase. Often they will repeat a word in a sentence or in the same paragraph. This is called the "echo effect" by some editors. An example is, She was a beautiful girl wearing a beautiful blue dress. We all have words that we use often, without being aware that we are doing so. To find those, use the edit feature on your computer and click on "Find." Type the word you suspect you have overused in the box next to the message, "Find What," then keep clicking on "Find Next" and search your manuscript for it, counting the times it is used. Here and there change it to a different word with the same meaning. This is where a good thesaurus comes in handy.

In writing a how-to book such as this one, some repetitions are necessary. There are issues touched upon in earlier chapters that need elaboration in others. For example, in the chapters on book proposals and query letters, I will be explaining some of the things mentioned before.

FLOW, CONTINUITY, AND TRANSITIONS

In writing, to flow means to proceed continuously, smoothly, or easily.

Continuity is defined as a continuous or connected whole.

A transition is a passage that links one scene or topic to another.

After you have done all the editing you can, read your entire manuscript through from start to finish at one sitting, if possible, keeping these guidelines in mind. Does it flow or are there words, phrases, or ideas that create snags along the way?

Do you keep going back and forth in time and, if so, is it really necessary? Maintaining a logical continuity helps the flow and makes it easier for the reader to follow.

When you begin a new sentence or paragraph, is it jarring, does it seem to skip a beat or to make too big a jump in the storyline? Is it too abrupt a change of subject? Good transitions can cure that problem.

William Zinsser advises, "Learn to alert the reader as soon as possible to any change in mood from the previous sentence. . . . Many of us were taught that no sentence should begin with 'but.' If that's what you learned, unlearn it—there's no stronger word at the start." I agree with him. You might have noticed that I start a lot of sentences in this book with *but* or *and*.

Transitions are also important when ending one chapter and starting another. Here's an example from *Island* by Aldous Huxley. At the end of chapter 14, a character named Susila is speaking:

"The *moksha*-medicine can take you to heaven; but it can also take you to hell. . . . And then beyond the beyond, back to where you started from—back to here, back to New Rothamsted, back to business as usual. Only now, of course, business as usual is completely different."

That last sentence hooks the reader and signals that something is about to change. Chapter 15 begins like this:

One, two, three, four . . . the clock in the kitchen struck twelve. How irrelevantly, seeing that time had ceased to exist!

Great writers know how to create page-turners. It would be hard to put *Island* down for the night after reading the last sentence of chapter 14. Huxley was a gifted storyteller but he was also a craftsman. And craft is something we can all learn even if creativity isn't.

Being aware of the above principles and making the necessary adjustments along the way can help make your writing more readable, interesting, and professional looking.

PUNCTUATION

Usage of quotations within quotations, and quotation marks with other punctuation marks, can be confusing. But here are some generally accepted rules.

Double quotation marks are used in text to enclose quoted words, phrases, and sentences. Single quotation marks are used for quotations within quotations. And quotations within those single quotation marks should be double quotation marks again. Here's an example:

> "Alice," Mom explained, "your dad didn't say you could borrow the car, period. He said, 'Alice may use the car only if she comes to me and says, "I'm sorry I dented the fender and I promise to get it fixed"!'"

The ending punctuation is placed according to the person it belongs to. Mom is saying what Dad said he wanted to hear Alice say. As the exclamation point belongs to Dad's speech, it goes inside the single quotation mark. There should be no other punctuation marks at the end. Hopefully, you will never be called upon to write something that makes punctuation so complicated.

Commas and periods, in the American style, are almost always placed inside the closing quotation mark. In rare instances where it is likely that there could be some confusion, it may be placed after the quotation mark. In the British style, if they belong to the quoted material, they are placed inside the quotation mark. If they belong to the including sentence as a whole, they are placed after the quotation mark. In any event, if you always place the comma or period inside the quotation mark, you will be right far more often than you'll be wrong. *The Chicago Manual of Style* recommends the American style of periods and commas.

> Where once we called people from that part of the world "Orientals," we now refer to them as "Asians."

Use commas to separate the elements in a series of three or more. When a conjunction joins the last two elements, use a comma before the conjunction.

Johnny, Suzie, Tom, and Jane attended his going-away party.

Most writers overuse the comma. Commas aren't necessary for clarity in a short sentence even when there is a prepositional phrase in the middle of it. But I see this often, especially when writers use grammar check. Not all of the suggestions in computer grammar programs are valid. Often these programs will suggest changes that are actually wrong for that particular usage. In general, use commas when they help to clarify the meaning. If the sentence can be read and understood correctly without the commas, omit them. After all, a comma indicates a pause and a pause slows down the pace.

A semicolon should be placed outside quotation marks or parentheses.

William Faulkner once said, "Really, the writer doesn't want success"; however, Faulkner certainly was successful.

There is rarely a reason to use a semicolon and it is a form of punctuation that seems to be going out of style. In most cases, a period and a new sentence will serve better. There are some instances when semicolons should be used for the sake of clarity, such as when items in a series involve internal punctuation.

The children's ages were as follows: Sara, thirteen; Joshua, twelve; Jimmy, nine; Alice, three; Joey, two; and Julie, nine months.

Exclamation points and question marks are usually placed inside quotation marks. For example:

Tina Turner's hit was "What's Love Got to Do with It?"

And from *Strange Fits of Passion* by William Wordsworth:

What fond and wayward thoughts will slide
Into a Lover's head!
"O mercy!" to myself I cried,
"If Lucy should be dead!"

Only rarely is the quotation mark placed before the ending punctuation. You may see this and it isn't necessarily wrong:

Who was called "The Voice"?

CAPITALIZATION AND ITALICIZATION

Names of places, regions, and localities should be capitalized: Middle East, East Coast, Great Plains, Golden Gate Bridge, Sunbelt. Also capitalize names of deities and sacred works: God, Jehovah, Allah, Zeus, Bible, Torah, Koran.

Titles of articles, short stories, and poems should be capitalized and in quotation marks. The following should be italicized: titles of books, plays, epic poems, magazines, newspapers, films, TV programs, major musical compositions, paintings, sculptures, foreign words and phrases, names of ships, aircraft, and space vehicles.

MAKE YOUR WRITING READER-FRIENDLY

Be concise and clear not only in the punctuation you use but in the words you choose. Even if you are writing a scholarly work, it will be a lot more interesting if you don't try to use every five-syllable word you know. Do you want to show off your vocabulary or do you want to communicate an idea? Consider this sentence:

Debilitating practices of procrastination, inappropriate decisions, and inconsistent productivity led to the administrative termination of the employee by the name of Oldham.

What did that mean and did you even care? It might be better to say *Oldham got fired because he put things off, made bad decisions, and wasn't very productive.* Another thing wrong with the sentence is that it is in the passive voice. The active voice is so much more interesting.

When you edit your work, see how many words you can take out. Fewer words, fewer syllables, and shorter sentences make better writing. That doesn't mean that your writing should consist entirely of short, choppy sentences. That's no good either. Vary the length of your sentences as well as your words.

There used to be a clear division between styles for writing and styles for speaking. That is no longer the case except in some forms of formal writing such as scientific papers and some academic works. But they could also gain by striving for simplicity and clarity over pedantry. Usually I edit manuscripts for books but occasionally I edit masters' theses and doctoral dissertations and I edit those differently. In these academic papers, the jargon of the profession is used and it is not only acceptable but preferred by most institutions. Although the style for academic papers is vastly different from that used in books intended for general readership, the sentences still should be comprehensible and uncomplicated. Clarity is always in style.

Styles have changed so much in the past decade or so that many of the rules we once followed are no longer valid.

In checking what the *Chicago Manual of Style*, fourteenth edition (published in 1993), had to say about split infinitives, I found this interesting footnote to section 2.98, *"Watching for errors and infelicities"*:

> The thirteenth edition [1982] of this manual included split infinitives among the examples of "errors and infelicities" but tempered the inclusion by adding, in parentheses, that they are "debatable 'error.'" The item has been dropped from the fourteenth edition because the Press now regards the intelligent and discriminating use of the construction as a legitimate form of expression and nothing writers or editors need feel uneasy about. Indeed, it seems to us that in many cases clarity and naturalness of expression are best served by a judicious splitting of infinitives.

We can now split infinitives, end sentences in prepositions, and even dangle participles without being in error as long as we are clear.

WORKING WITH AN EDITOR

Having someone with experience go over your work can be very beneficial. It's hard to be objective about your own writing and easy to overlook your own errors. Even though I am an editor, I need editing. My work is always improved after an editor has been through it.

If you decide to hire an editor, make sure that you get someone who is qualified. Find out if the editor has worked on books before. You may want to talk to authors who have worked with an editor on their books or get references from agents or publishers.

If you can't find someone with experience in editing books, an English teacher or a published writer might be good choices. Be aware, though, that not all English teachers are creative writers and not all writers can edit.

Ask what the editor charges and whether she is willing to edit a few pages so that you can see what kind of work she does. Don't expect anyone to do that free of charge. Make arrangements to pay her for three or four hours of work. Then she can get an idea of how long it will take to edit your entire book and can give you an estimate of the total charge. She should also be able to give you some excellent feedback at that point so that you may do some corrections yourself before you go on.

Getting an editor means you have to turn over your "baby" to someone who may not be as kind as you are to it. It's hard to keep our egos out of our writing. If you are arguing with the editor, any number of things may be going on. He may have overstepped his bounds and be making a lot of changes that don't work for you and your book. He may be too authoritarian, treating you as if you were his student, not his client. You may be trying to hold onto every word, closing your mind to changes that will improve your work. Or it could be that you are experiencing a personality conflict with the editor and he may not be the right one for you to work with. An editor should be clear, direct, and honest about how he thinks your work should be changed. However, there is no excuse for insensitivity or harsh, negative criticism. A good editor will make suggestions, not pronouncements.

The editor should not rewrite your book or change your voice. He should have the ability to guide you and help you organize your work. He should make grammatical, punctuation, and spelling corrections, and show you how you can improve the flow of your work.

How you relate to the editor will have an effect on the outcome of your manuscript. If you go into the relationship with the attitude that you want your book to be the best it can be, if you can remain open to his suggestions and keep your ego out of the process, you will very likely end up with a better manuscript than you started out with.

Whether you are working with an editor you hire or one who works for your publisher, recognize the fact that the editor is there to make you look good. A professional editor wants to help your book become the best it can be. Having the opportunity to discuss with the editor the changes he has suggested, whether or not you agree with them, can make you see your work in a new light and move your writing forward in giant steps.

My own experience with editors has been very good. The ones who worked on my books knew what they were doing and the edits and suggestions they made were excellent. My experiences on the other side of the fence, where I was the editor, have also been rewarding. As I don't take on clients or manuscripts I don't care for or don't feel qualified to work with, I nearly always enjoy the process. Writers are very interesting people, don't you think?

Chapter 8

The A-Plus Presentation

With regard to excellence, it is not enough to know, but we must try to have and use it.

—ARISTOTLE

The A-Plus Presentation involves excellence in appearance and attitude. Whether it is a query letter, a book proposal, a synopsis, a treatment, or your entire manuscript, it should be of high quality and presented in a professional manner. After all, your work is a part of you. It is one indication of who you are. Whenever you are speaking with an agent, publisher, or anyone in the publishing field, you need to present yourself as a professional, whether or not you have ever been paid for your writing. Even if this is the first book you have ever written, you are an expert in the area you are writing about—or you should be.

As you are preparing your work, consider the following principles of presentation. The principles apply to many areas of life, but these guidelines are specifically for you and your written works.

APPEARANCE

Your appearance is the first impression you will make, the first thing anyone sees. If you were looking for a job you would want to be neat, clean, and appropriately dressed. Your written presentation needs to be all of these as well. Often the overall appearance of your manuscript will determine whether your work will be taken seriously. The more professional looking your work is, the more likely it will be read. Here are some pointers:

- Always send fresh copies of your work. Do not send copies that have been returned to you from other presentations if they have been damaged or look shopworn. No one wants to think that she was not the first choice or important enough to warrant a good copy.
- Make generous margins. They should be at least one inch on all sides. This is more inviting to the eye and easier to read. Narrow margins make it look like you tried to cram a lot of information into a small space. Framed with wider margins, the page itself is more appealing.
- Although we are dealing primarily with manuscripts for books here, these principles apply to all kinds of writing. Present your work in the standard format for that genre.

For example: query letters should be single-spaced. Synopses for a proposed book are single-spaced. The other parts of the book proposal—the sample chapters and the pages of your manuscript—should be double-spaced.

A treatment (synopsis) for a TV or film script should be double-spaced, and it can be anywhere from three or four pages to thirty or forty, or even more.

There is a special format for television scripts for a half-hour taped series, a different script format for a TV "movie of the week" or a miniseries, and still a different format for theatrical film scripts. The script style for a stage play is different from all of the above. Generally, each page of a television or film script represents one minute of the taped or filmed show. A 120-page script, for example, corresponds to a two-hour-long film or TV show.

Do your research, get samples of these formats if you can, and pattern your presentation according to the standards of the industry, genre, and entity to which you are making your presentation.

- The print should be sharp and dark enough to read easily. If you can, avoid using a typewriter. Inkjet or laser printers are best. Use a font or typeface that is easy to read. Times New Roman or some variation of it is good. And it should be in at least 12 point. Anything smaller is also hard to read.
- Edit and proofread your work several times. Check it for misspellings, grammatical errors, overly long sentences or paragraphs, misplaced punctuation, and so forth.
- Don't send your work out the day you write it. Read it carefully again the next day or a week later to be sure that you are sending out your cleanest, clearest, and most interesting presentation.

SEND YOUR WORK TO THE RIGHT PUBLISHER

Publishers tell me that they get enormous numbers of misdirected proposals. Even if the presentation is professional, you don't have a chance if you are sending your work to a publisher who doesn't publish your kind of book. The same is true for literary agents. Many agents, like publishers, handle only specific genres of books. So choose carefully the person and company you send your query, book proposal, or manuscript to. Do your research to ascertain whether they are appropriate for what you have written. It will save the agent/publisher the time and trouble of dealing with an author who does not write what they represent/publish. It will also save you time, embarrassment, and money. When you figure in the cost of packaging, printing, and postage, it can cost a few dollars for each proposal you send out.

Then, when you do contact the agent or publisher, maintain a professional and courteous attitude.

ATTITUDE

The tone of your query letter and of any interview should be upbeat and positive. Be yourself but be the best self you can be. Here are some suggestions.

- Maintain a professional relationship with the agent or publisher you are dealing with. Stick to the facts of your works, career, and professional experience. Don't discuss personal problems. Don't gossip or bad-mouth his competitor (who may have already turned you down). People in the book publishing industry often know, talk to, and even like each other.
- Be friendly and open, not overly formal. Relax and let your personality come through.
- Be courteous. Even if the person you wish to impress isn't, even if she doesn't recognize the fact that you have written the best novel of the twenty-first century, and even if she doesn't have time to discuss your manuscript in depth. If the agent or publisher does not want your book, that's no reason to be rude. You may wish to present something else to this person someday. It would be wise to leave a good impression.
- Don't apologize and don't be defensive. If there is something in your work or your presentation of it that requires an elaborate explanation or an apology, then it isn't ready to be sent out. Keep all negative comments out of your communications. Maintain a positive attitude and it will show through in all that you do.
- Project confidence. It's not a good idea to praise your own work highly—how can you be objective when you are so close to it—but you can exhibit self-assurance and present yourself and your work in the best possible light.
- If you get a face-to-face meeting with a publisher, dress for business. That means no bare feet or cut-off jeans, no micromini skirts or low-cut blouses (no matter how well endowed you are), and no nose rings or green hair. Even though you are a writer and everyone knows that writers are eccentric, for this first meeting at least, be a little conservative in your appearance. Later, after your publisher has sold a million of your books, you can dress any way you like and he'll love you just the same.
- Be on time for your appointment whether it is for a telephone interview or a meeting in the agent's or publisher's office. If you are traveling to the meeting, leave yourself an extra half hour to get there. You never know what the traffic will be like. If you arrive more than fifteen minutes early, take a walk or stop at a

café to have a cup of coffee or tea and go over in your mind what you want to say. But don't have an alcoholic beverage even though you may think it will relax you. The alcohol could be detected on your breath and even if it isn't, it's best not to take the edge off. That edge could help you in your presentation. You don't want to be too mellow.

■ Be prepared. Bring an extra book proposal or manuscript with you just in case the one you sent was damaged or someone misplaced it and it can't be found. Anticipate questions the agent or publisher may ask. If you have obtained written permission to use certain material or quotes in your book, have it in your brief-case. Bring any photos, illustrations, charts, or graphs that were not included with your query letter, book proposal, or manuscript. Be prepared with names, addresses, and phone numbers of impor-tant sources, in case you are asked. Have a notepad and pen with you to take notes on what the agent or publisher says. Don't trust anything to memory.

■ Show enthusiasm but don't be emotional. Don't threaten to slash your wrists or their tires if they turn down your manuscript. No cursing, crying, begging, whining, or complaining. Neither anger nor self-pity will get you a publishing contract.

Okay, you probably already knew how to present yourself and you didn't need those tips. But not all writers are as stable as you. When I worked as assistant to television producers, I saw all of the above presentations at one time or other. And, believe it or not, publishers have told me that people actually have threatened to kill themselves if they couldn't get a book contract, and worse, they've threatened to kill the publisher. There are some pretty nutty people out there.

Once a publisher has indicated an interest in your book, be patient. When he says he will call you, assume the possibility exists that he really will. Give him a little time to do so. A week or two at least. After that, if you haven't heard, it's not inappropriate to call his office and ask about the status of your project.

If you have been asked by the acquisitions editor to do more research or to get permissions or endorsements, you have a good reason to contact her again to tell her that you have done so. But don't call every day and don't always ask to speak to the editor personally. She may be very busy. Her assistant will probably know the answers to your questions and can give you the information you want.

One more thing: don't get discouraged if this time things don't work out. If you got to speak to the agent or publisher directly, there must have been some interest there. Keep going. Keep sending out query letters and book proposals. Don't stop after three or four. It may take a dozen or a hundred contacts before you succeed.

Chapter 9

Copyright Information

Take away from English authors their copyrights, and you would very soon take away from England her authors.

—ANTHONY TROLLOPE

A copyright is a bundle of rights that provides authors and other creators of artistic works the sole right to grant or refuse permission to use their copyrighted works. When someone copies, adapts, or publishes a copyrighted work without permission, these rights are violated. Works published in the United States prior to January 1, 1923, are in the public domain, and works published after that are likely to be protected by copyright.

Violation of copyright can lead to serious civil and/or criminal penalties. There can be monetary damages of up to $150,000 per infringement for willfully copying or using copyrighted material. If a copyright owner finds it hard to prove the infringer amassed profits from the infringement, she can recover statutory damages of $750 to $30,000 (provided the works were registered before the start of the infringement). The damages almost always will vastly exceed what it would have cost to license the works.

Copyright law did not exist until the invention of the printing press in Europe in the fifteenth century. Before that it was expensive and very time-consuming to produce a book and few people knew how to read anyway.

By the middle of the sixteenth century, when books became cheaper and more widely available, the royal government of England granted a group of book publishers called the London Stationers' Company a monopoly on the printing of books. However, the purpose of this early form of copyright wasn't to protect authors' and publishers' rights. It was to raise revenue and give the government control over the contents of the publications. And it was effective. The publishers, not wishing to risk the loss of their monopoly, only published materials that were approved by the royal authorities.

THE HISTORY OF COPYRIGHT LAWS

The first real copyright law, in the modern sense, was passed in England in 1710. Called the Statute of Anne (named for Queen Anne), it granted authors the exclusive right to have their books printed for a limited duration. After twenty-eight years, the works could pass into public domain.

In 1790, the United States Congress adopted the nation's first copyright law. Congress made a major revision to it in the Copyright Act of 1909, reacting to new inventions such as photography and motion pictures. The 1909 Act was replaced by the Copyright Act of 1976 and, although the law has been amended often since then, this statute remains the legal basis for copyright protection in the United States.

Most nations have some form of copyright protection. The first international treaty was called the Berne Convention. It was adopted in Switzerland in 1886. Most of the countries in the world have signed this treaty and grant copyright protection to works of citizens of any member country. Although the Berne Convention is not actually an international copyright, it makes it easy for a creator to obtain copyright protection in other countries. The laws, however, are not always enforced and many countries violate the copyright protections. These violations have created a large market for counterfeit goods and unauthorized copies of books, music recordings, and videocassettes of films and television shows at very low prices.

SHOULD YOU REGISTER YOUR COPYRIGHT?

Yes. It offers you protections you can't get any other way. You may have heard that to prove authorship you can put your manuscript into a large manila envelope and send it to yourself. And when it arrives, don't open it, just file it away. That method of "protection," the so-called poor-man's copyright, may cost less than a copyright registration but I advise against it and so do attorneys. Why take a risk when the cost of registering your copyright officially is fairly nominal? If your manuscript has taken a year or two (or more) out of your life to write, doesn't it deserve the maximum legal protection you can give it?

Although fees were scheduled to go up in June 2002, the fee to register literary works (Form TX) remained at $30. However, that may change without much advance notice, so it is a good idea to check before you send in your copyright registration. To find out what current fees are, you can go to the Web site of the United States Copyright Office, listed later in this chapter.

THE ADVANTAGES OF COPYRIGHT REGISTRATION

There are some distinct advantages to registering your copyright with the Copyright Office:

- It establishes a public record of your copyright claim.
- Registration establishes *prima facie* evidence in court of the validity of the copyright.
- A timely registration will allow you (the copyright owner) to seek "statutory" damages—an amount between $750 and $30,000 per infringement—and attorney's fees. If the infringement had started before the work was registered, only the owner's actual damages and the infringer's profits are available to the author.
- The registration may be filed with the U.S. Customs Service to provide protection from the importation of infringing copies.

Mailing yourself a copy of your manuscript will not give you any of those protections. The above information and a great deal more can be found in Circular 1, Copyright Basics, published by the U.S. Copyright Office.

WHAT A COPYRIGHT IS

The Copyright Office describes a copyright as a form of protection provided by the law (title 17, U.S. Code) to authors of "original works of authorship" including literary, dramatic, musical, artistic, and certain other intellectual works. It is available both for published and unpublished works. Section 106 of the 1976 Copyright Act generally gives the owner of the copyright the exclusive right to do and to authorize others to do the following:

- Reproduce the copyrighted work in copies or phonorecords
- Prepare derivative works based upon the copyrighted work
- Distribute copies of it to the public by sale or other transfer of ownership, or by rental, lease, or lending
- Perform and/or display the copyrighted work publicly

It is illegal for anyone to violate any of the rights provided by the Copyright Office to the owner of copyright. These rights, however, are not unlimited in scope. One major limitation is the doctrine of "fair use." There are certain circumstances in which parts of a work may be quoted without your having to obtain permission. For more about this, see chapter 19, Ethics and Legal Concerns.

THE COPYRIGHT FORMS

The Copyright Office provides application forms for various types of registrations.

What we are concerned with here is Form TX and Short Form TX. These are the forms for registering nondramatic literary works including fiction, nonfiction, poetry, contributions to collective works, compilations, directories, catalogs, dissertations, theses, reports, speeches, bound or loose-leaf volumes, pamphlets, brochures, and single pages containing text.

You may obtain copies of these forms by writing the Copyright Office or by downloading them from its Web site. Any copies you make, however, must look like the original. They must be clear and printed back to back and head to head using both sides of a single sheet of white paper that is $8\frac{1}{2} \times 11$ inches in size. If you use the short form you don't have to be concerned with printing on the other side. The Short Form TX is one-sided.

Use Short Form TX if:

- You are the only author and copyright owner of the work
- The work is completely new
- The work was not made for hire
- You are not registering under a pseudonym or pen name

Send the following three items, all in one package:

1. One nonreturnable copy of your work
2. A completed application (Form TX)
3. A check or money order for the nonrefundable filing fee payable to Register of Copyrights

Send to the Library of Congress, Copyright Office, 101 Independence Avenue S.E., Washington, DC 20559-6000. You are not required to have your submission (manuscript) printed and you may use any paper size. To facilitate handling and long-term storage, it would be a good idea to staple, clip, or bind it in some way. This brings up another interesting provision of the copyright law called "mandatory deposit."

MANDATORY DEPOSIT REQUIREMENTS

To quote directly from Circular 7d, "All works under copyright protection and published in the United States on or after March 1, 1989, are subject to mandatory deposit whether published with or without a notice [of copyright]. . . . Section 704 of the Copyright Act states that these deposits 'are available to the Library of

Congress for its collections, or for exchange or transfer to any other library.' Section 407 of the copyright law requires the 'owner of copyright or of the exclusive right of publication' in a work published in the United States to deposit the required number of copies in the Copyright Office within three months of the date of such publication."

You are required to send two copies of the best edition of your copyrightable work. *Best edition* is defined as the copy of the highest quality. For example, if you have loose manuscript pages of your book as well as a bound edition, your "best edition" is the one that is bound.

Publication is defined in the copyright law as "the distribution of copies or phonorecords of a work to the public by sale or other transfer of ownership, or by rental, lease, or lending."

Deposits should be sent to:

Library of Congress
Register of Copyrights
Attn: 407 Deposits
101 Independence Avenue, S.E.
Washington, DC 20559-6000

The best course to satisfy the deposit requirements is by registering the copyright. This gives you the benefits of registration and also satisfies the mandatory deposit requirement. To register, you should send all of the following in the same package:

1. Two complete copies of the best edition of your work
2. A completed application (Form TX)
3. The nonrefundable filing fee (currently $30) payable to the Register of Copyrights

Although you will not be sent an acknowledgment that your application has been received, you may get a letter or phone call if they need additional information. Your certificate of registration will be sent within eight months to a year. Don't be concerned if it takes longer than that, however. Because of an anthrax scare in 2001 that shut the Copyright Office bureaus down for a period of time, they got behind in their work.

You may send your application package by registered or certified mail requesting a return receipt if you want to have proof that it arrived. If your registration is rejected, you will get a letter explaining why.

REGISTERING UNDER A PSEUDONYM OR PEN NAME

You may use a pseudonym or pen name when registering your copyright, but the pseudonym itself is not protected by copyright. If you are writing under a pseudonym but want to be identified by your legal name in the copyright records, give your legal name followed by your pseudonym in space 2, "Name and Address of Author and Owner of the Copyright." For example, Samuel Clemens would fill in space 2 as follows: "Samuel Langhorne Clemens whose pseudonym is Mark Twain."

Also check "yes" in the box next to "Pseudonymous?" at space 2. If you do not wish your identity revealed in the records, give your pseudonym and identify it as such (example: "Mark Twain, pseudonym"). You may also leave the space blank, but you still must identify the citizenship or domicile of the author.

You may use a pseudonym in space 4 but do not leave this space blank. However, be warned that if you hold your copyright under a fictitious name, you may have problems proving ownership in any business dealings. It's best to consult an attorney in this case. And you *must* sign Form TX in space 8. *Do not* use Short Form TX.

Copyright Office fees are subject to change.
For current fees, check the Copyright Office
website at *www.copyright.gov*, write the Copyright Office, or call (202) 707-3000.

FORM TX

For a Nondramatic Literary Work
UNITED STATES COPYRIGHT OFFICE

REGISTRATION NUMBER

TX   TXU

EFFECTIVE DATE OF REGISTRATION

Month   Day   Year

DO NOT WRITE ABOVE THIS LINE. IF YOU NEED MORE SPACE, USE A SEPARATE CONTINUATION SHEET.

1

TITLE OF THIS WORK ▼

PREVIOUS OR ALTERNATIVE TITLES ▼

PUBLICATION AS A CONTRIBUTION If this work was published as a contribution to a periodical, serial, or collection, give information about the collective work in which the contribution appeared.   **Title of Collective Work ▼**

If published in a periodical or serial give: **Volume ▼**   **Number ▼**   **Issue Date ▼**   **On Pages ▼**

2   a

NAME OF AUTHOR ▼

DATES OF BIRTH AND DEATH
Year Born ▼   Year Died ▼

Was this contribution to the work a "work made for hire"?
☐ Yes
☐ No

AUTHOR'S NATIONALITY OR DOMICILE
Name of Country
OR { Citizen of ▶
Domiciled in▶

WAS THIS AUTHOR'S CONTRIBUTION TO THE WORK
Anonymous?   ☐ Yes ☐ No
Pseudonymous? ☐ Yes ☐ No
If the answer to either of these questions is "Yes," see detailed instructions.

NATURE OF AUTHORSHIP Briefly describe nature of material created by this author in which copyright is claimed. ▼

NOTE

Under the law, the "author" of a "work made for hire" is generally the employer, not the employee (see instructions). For any part of this work that was "made for hire" check "Yes" in the space provided, give the employer (or other person for whom the work was prepared) as "Author" of that part, and leave the space for dates of birth and death blank.

b

NAME OF AUTHOR ▼

DATES OF BIRTH AND DEATH
Year Born ▼   Year Died ▼

Was this contribution to the work a "work made for hire"?
☐ Yes
☐ No

AUTHOR'S NATIONALITY OR DOMICILE
Name of Country
OR { Citizen of ▶
Domiciled in▶

WAS THIS AUTHOR'S CONTRIBUTION TO THE WORK
Anonymous?   ☐ Yes ☐ No
Pseudonymous? ☐ Yes ☐ No
If the answer to either of these questions is "Yes," see detailed instructions.

NATURE OF AUTHORSHIP Briefly describe nature of material created by this author in which copyright is claimed. ▼

c

NAME OF AUTHOR ▼

DATES OF BIRTH AND DEATH
Year Born ▼   Year Died ▼

Was this contribution to the work a "work made for hire"?
☐ Yes
☐ No

AUTHOR'S NATIONALITY OR DOMICILE
Name of Country
OR { Citizen of ▶
Domiciled in▶

WAS THIS AUTHOR'S CONTRIBUTION TO THE WORK
Anonymous?   ☐ Yes ☐ No
Pseudonymous? ☐ Yes ☐ No
If the answer to either of these questions is "Yes," see detailed instructions.

NATURE OF AUTHORSHIP Briefly describe nature of material created by this author in which copyright is claimed. ▼

3   a

YEAR IN WHICH CREATION OF THIS WORK WAS COMPLETED This information must be given ◀ Year in all cases.

b **DATE AND NATION OF FIRST PUBLICATION OF THIS PARTICULAR WORK**
Complete this information ONLY if this work has been published.
Month ▶ _____ Day▶ _____ Year▶ _____ ◀ Nation

4

See instructions before completing this space.

COPYRIGHT CLAIMANT(S) Name and address must be given even if the claimant is the same as the author given in space 2. ▼

TRANSFER If the claimant(s) named here in space 4 is (are) different from the author(s) named in space 2, give a brief statement of how the claimant(s) obtained ownership of the copyright. ▼

APPLICATION RECEIVED

ONE DEPOSIT RECEIVED

TWO DEPOSITS RECEIVED

FUNDS RECEIVED

DO NOT WRITE HERE
OFFICE USE ONLY

MORE ON BACK ▶   • Complete all applicable spaces (numbers 5-9) on the reverse side of this page.
• See detailed instructions.   • Sign the form at line 8.

DO NOT WRITE HERE
Page 1 of _____ pages

	EXAMINED BY	FORM TX
	CHECKED BY	
	☐ CORRESPONDENCE Yes	FOR COPYRIGHT OFFICE USE ONLY

DO NOT WRITE ABOVE THIS LINE. IF YOU NEED MORE SPACE, USE A SEPARATE CONTINUATION SHEET.

PREVIOUS REGISTRATION Has registration for this work, or for an earlier version of this work, already been made in the Copyright Office?
☐ Yes ☐ No If your answer is "Yes," why is another registration being sought? (Check appropriate box.) ▼

a. ☐ This is the first published edition of a work previously registered in unpublished form.

b. ☐ This is the first application submitted by this author as copyright claimant.

c. ☐ This is a changed version of the work, as shown by space 6 on this application.

If your answer is "Yes," give: **Previous Registration Number** ▶   **Year of Registration** ▶

5

DERIVATIVE WORK OR COMPILATION
Preexisting Material Identify any preexisting work or works that this work is based on or incorporates. ▼   a

6

See instructions before completing this space.

Material Added to This Work Give a brief, general statement of the material that has been added to this work and in which copyright is claimed. ▼   b

DEPOSIT ACCOUNT If the registration fee is to be charged to a Deposit Account established in the Copyright Office, give name and number of Account.
Name ▼   **Account Number** ▼   a

7

CORRESPONDENCE Give name and address to which correspondence about this application should be sent.   Name/Address/Apt/City/State/ZIP ▼   b

Area code and daytime telephone number ▶   Fax number ▶

Email ▶

CERTIFICATION* I, the undersigned, hereby certify that I am the
                                          Check only one ▶
☐ author
☐ other copyright claimant
☐ owner of exclusive right(s)
☐ authorized agent of _____

of the work identified in this application and that the statements made
by me in this application are correct to the best of my knowledge.

Name of author or other copyright claimant, or owner of exclusive right(s) ▲

8

Typed or printed name and date ▼ If this application gives a date of publication in space 3, do not sign and submit it before that date.

_____ Date ▶ _____

Handwritten signature (X) ▼

X _

Certificate will be mailed in window envelope to this address:	Name ▼
	Number/Street/Apt ▼
	City/State/ZIP ▼

YOU MUST:
• Complete all necessary spaces
• Sign your application in space 8

SEND ALL 3 ELEMENTS IN THE SAME PACKAGE:
1. Application form
2. Nonrefundable filing fee in check or money order payable to *Register of Copyrights*
3. Deposit material

Fees are subject to change. For current fees, check the Copyright Office website at www.copyright.gov, write the Copyright Office, or call (202) 707-3000.

MAIL TO:
Library of Congress
Copyright Office
101 Independence Avenue, S.E.
Washington, D.C. 20559-6000

9

*17 U.S.C. § 506(e): Any person who knowingly makes a false representation of a material fact in the application for copyright registration provided for by section 409, or in any written statement filed in connection with the application, shall be fined not more than $2,500.

Rev: June 2002—20,000 Web Rev: June 2002 ♻ Printed on recycled paper   U.S. Government Printing Office: 2000-461-113/20,021

Copyright Office fees are subject to change. For current fees, check the Copyright Office website at *www.copyright.gov*, write the Copyright Office, or call (202) 707-3000.

SHORT FORM TX
For a Nondramatic Literary Work

UNITED STATES COPYRIGHT OFFICE

Registration Number

TX   TXU

Effective Date of Registration

Application Received

Examined By

Deposit Received
One   Two

Correspondence

Fee Received

TYPE OR PRINT IN BLACK INK. DO NOT WRITE ABOVE THIS LINE.

Title of This Work: **1**

Alternative title or title of larger work in which this work was published:

Name and Address of Author and Owner of the Copyright: **2**

Nationality or domicile:
Phone, fax, and email:

Phone ( )   Fax ( )
Email

Year of Creation: **3**

If work has been published, **Date and Nation of Publication:**   **4**

a. Date _____   (Month, day, and year all required)
          Month   Day   Year
b. Nation

Type of Authorship in This Work: **5**

Check all that this author created.

❑ Text (includes fiction, nonfiction, poetry, computer programs, etc.)
❑ Illustrations
❑ Photographs
❑ Compilation of terms or data

Signature: **6**

Registration cannot be completed without a signature.

I certify that the statements made by me in this application are correct to the best of my knowledge. Check one:
❑ Author ❑ Authorized agent

X _

OPTIONAL

Name and Address of Person to Contact for Rights and Permissions: **7**

Phone, fax, and email:

❑ Check here if same as #2 above.

Phone ( )   Fax ( )
Email

8

Certificate will be mailed in window envelope to this address:

Name ▼

Number/Street/Apt ▼

City/State/ZIP ▼

Complete this space only if you currently hold a Deposit Account in the Copyright Office.

9

Deposit Account #_____
Name _____

DO NOT WRITE HERE   Page 1 of _____ pages

*17 U.S.C. § 506(e): Any person who knowingly makes a false representation of a material fact in the application for copyright registration provided for by section 409, or in any written statement filed in connection with the application, shall be fined not more than $2,500.

Rev: June 2002—20,000   Web Rev: June 2002   ♻ Printed on recycled paper

U.S. Government Printing Office: 2000-461-113/20,021

What Cannot Be Copyrighted?

- Works that have not been fixed in a tangible form of expression, such as improvised speeches, dances, or music that has not been written or recorded
- Ideas, procedures, methods, systems, processes, concepts, principles, discoveries or devices, as distinguished from a description, explanation, or illustration
- Titles, names, short phrases and slogans, familiar symbols or designs, variations of lettering or coloring, lists of ingredients or contents
- Works consisting entirely of information that is common property and containing no original authorship, such as calendars, height and weight charts, tape measures and rulers, and lists or tables taken from public documents or other common sources

Copyrighting Recipes

A question that comes up often is: If a list of ingredients in a recipe can't be copyrighted, what protection does a cookbook author have? According to the Copyright Office, when a recipe is "accompanied by substantial literary expression in the form of an explanation or directions, or when there is a combination of recipes, as in a cookbook, there may be a basis for copyright protection." Protection extends only to "original works of authorship" that are fixed in a tangible form. The author must have "produced the work by his own intellectual effort, as distinguished from copying an existing work."

So if you are writing a cookbook that contains original recipes and you want to register the copyright, be sure to include, along with the lists of ingredients, your directions or instructions for preparing each recipe. For more information, get "Copyright Registration of Recipes," FL 122, from the Copyright Office.

Is a Notice of Copyright Required?

Under U.S. law a copyright notice is no longer required but it is still a good idea to indicate that your work is copyrighted. Use of the notice identifies the copyright owner and the first year of publication. If a proper notice of copyright appears on the published work, no one can claim they didn't know the work was protected.

The use of the copyright notice is your responsibility. You don't need permission from the Copyright Office to use it. And you do not have to register it first. The notice should contain the following:

- The symbol © or the word "Copyright" or the abbreviation "Copr." and
- The year of first publication of the work, and
- The name of the owner of the copyright (example: © 2003 Jane Doe)

HOW TO REACH THE COPYRIGHT OFFICE

For general information, you may call the Copyright Public Information Office at (202) 707-3000 between the hours of 8:30 a.m. and 5:00 p.m. Eastern time, Monday through Friday.

- Application forms and circulars are available on their Web site, *www.copyright.gov*. They may be downloaded and printed.
- If you have questions, you may call the Forms and Publications Hotline at (202) 707-9100.
- Information by fax (but not application forms) is available by Fax-on-Demand at (202) 707-2600.
- For information by regular mail, write to the Library of Congress, Copyright Office Publications Section, LM-455, 101 Independence Avenue S.E., Washington, DC 20559-6000.

Chapter 10

Literary Agents

For many authors, an agent agreement is the first agree-
ment they will ever face in their literary endeavors . . . it
is critical to remember that the agent works for the author
and not the reverse.

—"UNDERSTANDING THE AUTHOR-AGENCY RELATIONSHIP"
(A BOOKLET PUBLISHED BY THE NATIONAL WRITERS UNION)

As in all professions, there are good agents and there are bad agents. A bad agent is worse than none at all. Before you begin looking for a literary agent, you should know a few facts so that you can determine whether having representation will be in your best interests. The type of book you are writing and the ways in which it will be distributed may influence your decision. You may find that an agent is unnecessary and may only get in your way.

If you decide that you must have an agent, this chapter will provide you with information on finding a qualified agent who is best suited for you and your work.

DO YOU NEED AN AGENT?

The answer to that question depends on several factors. If you already have access to a publisher or publishers who are likely to want to publish your book you may not need an agent. If you plan to contact small publishers, an agent might only get in the way. Smaller houses will accept queries and book proposals from individual authors, and, in fact, some prefer to deal with an author who does not have an agent. However, if you want to reach a major publisher such as Simon & Schuster or Random House you will probably need an agent to represent you. Large publishing houses rarely deal directly with an author before the contract is signed.

If you choose not to have a literary agent represent you and you know the book-publishing business well, you may prefer to represent yourself. However, you should have an attorney who specializes in intellectual property and/or entertainment law look over any publishing contract that is offered you. You may want to do that even if you do have an agent, because the contract may be complex and beyond the area of expertise of an agent. Although you would have to pay a lawyer a fee, you wouldn't have to share your royalties with an attorney as you would with an agent. However, many lawyers won't review book contracts unless the dollar amounts are large. One of the benefits of membership in the National Writers Union is free contract advice for writers dealing with an agent or publisher. They also provide members with the NWU Preferred Literary Agent Agreement.

The decision to retain an agent is a major one in your career. It is important for you to know as much as you can about the agent you choose and to understand the agency agreement. Whether or not you have an agent, you should participate in all the decisions that affect your life as an author and educate yourself at every level of your career. Knowledge is power.

The big advances you may have heard about in the past are things of the past. The new reality is that even major publishers do not offer large advances anymore unless you are a famous person or a proven author whose books regularly sell in the thousands or hundreds of thousands.

Since the smaller publishers often do not give authors any advance, most agents are reluctant to represent an author who will appeal only to small publishers. Fifteen percent of nothing is still nothing. The agent won't realize any financial remuneration until your royalties start to roll in—and that could take years.

There are clear advantages and disadvantages to having a literary agent.

THE ADVANTAGES

Agents are more likely to get you an offer from a publisher than you are yourself. After all, that is their specialty. They will probably get you a larger advance and bigger royalties than you could negotiate for yourself, as well as a more advantageous contract all around. Qualified agents know what to watch for in a publishing contract and how to protect your rights. Jonathan Kirsch, an attorney specializing in intellectual property matters and publishing law, and author of *Kirsch's Guide to the Book Contract,* advises:

> An experienced agent will be far more adept, insightful and effective in dealing with the legal technicalities of a book contract than an attorney who lacks long and specific experience in the book publishing industry.

Experienced agents know which publishers buy the kind of book you are writing. They may already have a relationship with particular publishers through placing other books with them. Good agents may also nurture new authors and help guide their careers.

THE DISADVANTAGES

One obvious disadvantage is that you will probably be required to give the agent 15 percent of your advance and royalties. For example, if she negotiates an advance of $5,000, you will receive $4,250 and she will get $750. The money won't come directly to you. The check is mailed to your agent who takes her percentage out and then sends you a check for the remaining amount. The same is true for your royalty checks, which are usually sent twice a year.

Once you have signed with an agent, you may not be able to deal with publishers on your own. So even though you may have contacts within a particular publishing company, you may have trouble working with them without first getting the approval of your agent. If you have signed an agreement with the agent for representation for a period of two years and the agent does nothing for you, it may be complicated for you to get out of that relationship.

Some literary agents specialize in representing authors of books and may not have any connections with the television or film industry. If they don't have experience analyzing and negotiating TV and film deals, you may need a separate agent for that. If you have written a script or a treatment (synopsis) for a proposed film or television production it would be better for you to find an agent who deals mainly with that industry and is signatory to the Writers Guild of America (WGA).

How Do Agents Get New Clients?

There are several ways agents get clients. These are the major ones, in order of frequency and likelihood.

- Through referrals. These may come from existing clients, editors, other agents, published authors, or experts in a particular field.
- Through their speaking engagements at writers' conferences and seminars.
- Through written queries from authors.

If you have met an agent through a seminar, a business associate, or some other way in which you have made personal contact, it is not inappropriate to call and ask if you may send a query letter. If the agent is not too busy, you may even have the opportunity to pitch your idea over the phone.

How Do You Find an Agent?

To look for an agent, check *Literary Market Place,* published by R. R. Bowker, or *Guide to Literary Agents,* published by Writer's Digest Books. *Writer's Market,* published by Writer's Digest Books, and *The Writer's Handbook,* published by The Writer Inc. now list agents but the listings are not extensive.

An agent is not necessarily qualified just because he is listed in the above guides. Some of them may be "business card" agents and may not be experienced or reputable. Literary agents are not like attorneys or building contractors. They don't have to pass exams, adhere to any rules, or prove their level of competence. They don't need a license from any regulatory agency. They can simply print up business cards and call themselves literary agents. Their listing, though, is a starting point in your search for someone to represent you, because it will tell you what kinds of books they work with.

Get the latest issue of the guides, because agents move, go out of business, or become otherwise unavailable from year to year. Some of the above publications have Web sites and you may be able to do much of your research over the Internet.

Like publishers, many agents specialize in particular genres such as how-to, spirituality, health, and mysteries. Because nonfiction books are easier to sell than novels, especially by first-time authors, most agents represent nonfiction writers. If you are a novelist, you may have a tougher time finding a literary agent. The closer you can match the agent to the type of book you are writing, the better chance you will have that she will be interested in representing you and your book.

Before you contact any agents, notice whether they want to be queried first or will accept a synopsis or a book proposal along with your query or cover letter. Very few will want to look at a complete manuscript on first contact.

HOW DO YOU CHOOSE THE *RIGHT* AGENT?

Whenever possible, get recommendations from authors, publishers, editors, or others who have dealt with the agent.

An agent may suggest that your manuscript would have a better chance of being accepted by a publisher if you have it edited. That may be a valid comment as most manuscripts do need professional editing. But beware if the agent refers you to a specific company. Some agents receive referral fees from editorial companies and may be more interested in collecting their fee than in helping you. Those agents may not agree to represent you even after your book has been edited by someone they recommended. You could spend a lot of money on an editor who is not even right for your book and still end up without an agent.

For information on qualified agents, check with the Association of Authors' Representatives (AAR) and the National Writers Union (NWU), both of which require literary agents to be qualified and to abide by a high standard of ethics to be listed with them. The Writers Guild of America also requires the agents to prove their experience and qualifications in order to be a signatory to their organization.

WHAT TO WATCH OUT FOR

Some agents charge a reading fee of up to $450. As that may be a major source of income for them rather than a percentage of your advance and royalties, they may not be operating in your best interests.

Although the AAR does not accept agents who charge reading fees, there are a few fee-charging agents who are legitimate and render a valuable service to writers. But picking a good one out of the crowd is hard to do. If an agent merely reads your manuscript and then passes on it you will have learned nothing. Some agents will send a report and then ask for an additional fee for a more detailed analysis. That practice is highly suspect. If you think you have found a responsible, ethical, fee-charging agent and decide to send your material to her, be sure that you will get something in return. Ask the following questions:

- What services do you provide for the reading fee?
- Will my material be evaluated by someone with professional experience?
- Will I receive a detailed report with some editorial suggestions and the marketability for this type of book?
- How long before I receive a report?
- What is the fee for a complete analysis?
- If you decide to accept me as a client will the fee be refunded?

Don't be afraid to ask the agent for information about her charges, method of working, and experience, as well as a list of her clients' published books. Remember, the agent is paid by you, not the other way around. You have a right to know everything about her that will help you in your selection.

It is important to choose an agent who is not only ethical and experienced but is someone you feel rapport with. The National Writers Union gets many complaints from writers who have been defrauded and mistreated by agents. Many so-called agents are nothing but scam artists.

Script agents are in a different category from literary agents. Those who are signatory to the Writers Guild of America cannot charge more than a 10 percent commission and they must abide by a standard code of behavior.

Although it will be helpful to get a list of approved agents from the Association of Authors' Representatives, there are other organizations as well that can give you valuable information on specific agents. The National Writers Union maintains an Agent Database available to NWU members. Many working writers join the NWU because of the benefits and protections they offer. The Agent Research & Evaluation Company tracks agents in court records and the press. They've been around since 1980 and have a good reputation. They sell reports from their database and you can get a summary of an agent's activities from them. The American Society of Journalists and Authors reports problems with agents from time to time in their Contract Watch.

The above, along with contact information, are listed in Resources in the back of this book.

Once you have decided on which agents to query—and you may want to choose several—you can begin to compose your letter, customizing it to fit each particular agent. (See chapter 12, The Query Letter.)

Chapter 11

The Book Proposal

Oh, that my words were now written! Oh, that they were printed in a book.

—JOB 19:23

Have you ever said, "But I'm an author—an artist—my job is to write. Why do I need to prepare a book proposal?" I think most writers feel that way. I certainly do. In a perfect world, we could be authors who just write and get discovered by publishers who sell thousands of our books and make us rich and famous. Unfortunately, we live in an imperfect world. We have to work at making ourselves known to those who are in the business of publishing the kinds of books we write. We need to convince publishers that they will benefit by publishing our book. But even that isn't enough. We will then have to convince book buyers that they will enjoy reading it. That means we need to do a book proposal.

A BOOK PROPOSAL IS LIKE A BUSINESS PLAN

Suppose you had invented a robotic maid and wanted it to be carried by a department store chain that would sell it to its customers. But the stores already carry a robotic maid in their housewares section—several brands, in fact. What's different and better about yours? Well, like the others, yours cleans the house but, unlike the others, it also does windows. Not only that, yours makes lunch and laughs at your jokes. But the people in that department store who make the decisions aren't going to know all that unless you tell them. You could give them a call but before they will make a commitment, they'll have to know more details. They are going to want to see some promotional material, the product itself, and possibly a demonstration. They'll have to be convinced that there are people out there who are just dying to have your particular robotic maid. It's your job to sell them on this wondrous machine.

It's not that much different when your product is a book. Writing a query letter isn't enough. It may get a publisher interested but he will still want a demonstration. He will want to know more about your book and whether there is a market for it. He'll ask to see a book proposal and sample chapters or, sometimes, the entire manuscript.

For a nonfiction book, you can think of an idea, research the market, gather the facts, organize the material, write two or three chapters, and prepare a book proposal to send to a publisher before you even write the book. Then, if a publisher likes what he sees he may offer an advance. If you are like most writers, you have to earn a living. Having a cash advance might allow you to take a leave of absence from your job so that you can spend the time it takes to complete the book. The acquisitions editor of the publishing company will probably have some ideas of his own regarding what he wants to see in your book and will give you input to help you write a book that has a good chance of selling a lot of copies.

An excellent resource is *Write the Perfect Book Proposal* by Jeff Herman and Deborah M. Adams. One of the features I particularly like about this book is, as its subtitle says, it contains "10 Proposals That Sold and Why." In their introduction, the authors state:

> Thousands of writers each year fail to find a publisher because they write mediocre proposals, even though many of them would have gone on to write successful books. The proposal process must be taken seriously. It's the price of admission to being a published author.

While the query letter for a novel and a nonfiction book are essentially the same in principle, the book proposal format presented here is designed primarily for the nonfiction book.

A book proposal for fiction does not contain as many parts. The proposal for a novel might have only the title page, a synopsis, and an author bio. If the author has written other books they should be listed, along with information on how well they sold. Although there are exceptions, most agents and publishers want to see the entire manuscript of a novel rather than sample chapters. A novel is a much tougher sell than a nonfiction book.

A query letter should not be sent out until your book proposal has been completed. If you get a request from an agent or publisher to see your proposal, it should be ready so that you can send it right away. Interest may evaporate if you let a few weeks or months go by.

The advantages of writing a book proposal before you write the book are many. As you go through all the steps of the proposal you will learn:

- **How to focus on your subject.** If you have a descriptive title and can sum up your book in one short sentence, you probably have a clear idea of what your book is about.
- **How to describe your book to others.** By writing a synopsis, you will be able to get to the essence of the information contained in your book and explain it clearly.
- **How to organize your material.** Preparing a chapter-by-chapter outline of your book will help keep you on track as you write.
- **Whether you have a salable idea.** As you research the market potential, you will find out if your book is likely to find a wide audience.
- **How to sell yourself.** You will discover your qualifications for writing your book when you tell about your background and promotional skills. You can then build upon your strengths and do additional research in areas where you lack training or experience.
- **What your competition is** and if there are other books on the same subject. If you find books that are similar to yours, you may want to change yours in some way to make it stand out from the

rest. You may even need to rethink whether you want to write this particular book at all.

Whether you have already written a nonfiction book or are contemplating writing one you will need to know what it takes to sell it. A book proposal can be prepared no matter what stage of writing you are currently in. There are several factors that make for a bestselling nonfiction book. If you address all of these issues carefully and your book meets most of the following criteria, your chances of getting published will be greatly improved.

WHAT MAKES A NONFICTION BOOK SUCCESSFUL?

- The subject is timely and/or timeless; it is unique or presented in a unique way; it is interesting and appeals to a wide audience.
- The title is descriptive; it is intriguing or seductive, shocks or soothes, or in some way attracts attention.
- It is well written and carefully edited with attention paid to spelling, grammar, and sentence structure.
- It avoids scientific or technical terminology unfamiliar to the layperson. It is easy to read.
- The author is a professional in the field about which he is writing, is considered an authority on the subject, or has done extensive research on it.
- The material is well organized.
- The presentation is attractive, appealing, and professional looking.
- It has been diligently promoted and marketed.

Prepare your book proposal with all of the above factors in mind. The last item may not seem to be of concern to you as the author. But it is, because you will have to help promote and, in some cases, market your book no matter who the publisher is.

The format may differ somewhat depending on the publisher or agent to whom you will be presenting your proposal. For instance, some publishers require one sample chapter, some three or even more.

Some may ask that you put your name on every page and others may ask you not to. It's a good idea to modify your book proposal according to the wishes of the person or company with whom you are dealing. You can find this information in a number of ways:

- By checking the publisher's listing in the latest issue of Writer's Market or The Writer's Handbook to see if they give this information
- By writing to the publishing company and asking for guidelines
- By checking out the publisher's Web site
- By e-mailing the acquisitions editor
- By calling the publishing company on the phone and asking

More and more, publishers are accepting queries and book proposals over the Internet. Their listing in one of the above reference books may tell you whether you can make submissions by e-mail. That information might also be on their Web site.

The entire book proposal, except for the synopsis, should be double-spaced. On each page, place the section number and subject in the upper right corner. Below that put the title of your book and under that, the page number in that section.

THE BOOK PROPOSAL CONTENTS PAGE

It is helpful to have a table of contents that shows at a glance what you have included in your proposal. At the top of the page, type "Book Proposal for [the title of your book]." Below that list the sections of the book proposal you have included, a list of illustrations, if any, and note which illustrations you are enclosing. After that, state which chapters you are sending. On the following page is an example.

BOOK PROPOSAL FOR

_____

(title of book)

_____

(subtitle)

by _____

(name of author)

      I.   Title Page
      II.   Synopsis
      III. About the Author
      IV. Market Potential
      V.   Competitive Works
      VI. Chapter Outline
      VII. List of Illustrations

Sample Illustrations
(note what illustrations are included)

Chapters _____
(note the chapter numbers included)

Author's name
Address
City, State and Zip
Telephone and fax number
E-mail address

I. TITLE PAGE (TITLE AND BRIEF DESCRIPTION OF BOOK)

Your title should be provocative and succinct. Publishers usually prefer short titles and they are easier for potential readers to remember. Notice how many books on best-seller lists have three-word titles. Although there are some exceptions, such as *Men Are from Mars, Women Are from Venus* and *How to Get What You Want and Want What You Have,* only rarely do books on those lists have more than six words in the title. You can add a subtitle if you think that your short title doesn't tell enough about the book.

Do your best to get a hook into the title—something that will grab a reader's attention. Engage the emotions as much as possible, as these titles do: *Yesterday I Cried, Memoirs of a Geisha, All Too Human, We'll Meet Again,* and *Think and Grow Rich.*

The title should convey in some way what your book is about, especially if it is nonfiction. Some examples of titles that do this are: *Emotional Intelligence, Dr. Atkin's New Diet Revolution, Slaves in the Family, The Greatest Generation,* and *Ageless Body, Timeless Mind.*

Study the subject guide to *Books in Print* and note whether the subject you are writing on has been updated within the past few years. Also check *Forthcoming Books,* which details the books that publishers currently have in the works. Both are published by R. R. Bowker Co. Many bookstores and public libraries have these lists on their computer.

Choose a title that has not been used before. Even though you can use an existing title because titles cannot be copyrighted, you wouldn't want your book confused with someone else's. If you want yours to stand out, it's best to select a title that is unique. If there are several books on the subject you have chosen, be sure that yours is different in important ways.

On the title page, put your title, subtitle (if any), and your name as the author. Below that write a brief description of your book. This is your primary sales pitch. Make it short and intriguing.

List the number of words you have written or expect to write. An average double-spaced manuscript page has around 300 to

350 words. The number of words on a book page varies widely depending on the size of the font and the page and the width of the margins. Most nonfiction books are between 170 and 300 pages. If your book will have fewer or more pages than these, be sure that there is a good reason for it. If there are fewer pages, don't pad. Every word should have a reason to be there. If there are more than 300 pages, be sure that you have not repeated yourself and that it requires that many pages to make all your points concisely.

Number the pages of the book proposal according to the section they are in, starting with page one in each new section.

On the following page is an example of a title page.

I. TITLE PAGE
A Woman's Way

A Woman's Way
The Stop-Smoking Book for Women

By Mary Embree

Smoking is a greater health hazard for women than
for men and it is harder for women to quit.

Number of words: 40,000

II. SYNOPSIS

This is an overview or brief summary of the book. It should be about one-and-a-half to two pages long and single-spaced. Place the book proposal section number and name in the top right corner of the page. Below that put the title of your book, and under that the page number.

Example:

II. SYNOPSIS
Title of Book
Page 1

Having a focused idea and being able to explain it in a few short paragraphs is essential. Tell the purpose of your book and what it will do for the reader.

The lead paragraph must grab the interest of the publishing company's acquisitions editor. Open with a powerful statement, startling statistics, or facts that will create interest or an emotional reaction.

Read book reviews, especially those on a subject similar to yours, and study book jackets as guides in developing the tone of the synopsis. As some agents and acquisitions editors may not read beyond this point, it is important that you make the synopsis not only informative but interesting.

The synopsis should have a beginning, middle, and end, just as your book does. Tell how your book opens, what it is about, and how it ends. You may want to give some of the highlights, specific events, dialogue, or unknown facts.

At the bottom of the page, estimate the time needed to complete the book once the contract is signed.

Try to touch on most of the following in your synopsis:

■ What kind of book is it? Tell whether it is a how-to book, a mystery, children's book, book of poetry, cookbook, historical novel, biography, etc.

- If it is a novel, what is the story? Who are the main characters?
- What is interesting and different about it? Is there an unusual twist? A unique point of view?
- How is it written? For example, if it is a novel, is it written in first person? If a nonfiction book, is it written for the layperson?

III. ABOUT THE AUTHOR

This is also called Author's Background and Promotional Skills, or Biographical Information. It is a narrative statement of your qualifications, experience, and reasons for writing the book. Do not send a résumé or curriculum vitae. Your bio should be no more than two pages long.

Tell about yourself, list other books you have written, and explain your promotional skills such as public speaking, television or radio appearances, or seminars you have conducted on the subject. Suggest the names of prominent figures or authorities who may endorse your book. If you already have contacted them and they have agreed, be sure to mention it.

To see if you have covered everything, use the following checklist:

❑ Education; special training.
❑ Experience in the field you are writing about.
❑ Other books, articles, scripts, or papers you have written.
❑ Public speaking experience. Seminar presenter? Teacher? Politician? Actor?
❑ Personal information, especially when applicable to what you are writing.
❑ Marketing or promotional experience.
❑ Reason for writing this book.
❑ Endorsements.

All of the above may not apply to you and your book. If you are writing a novel, a university degree may be unimportant. If you are writing a nonfiction book regarding a specific field of interest it will be important to show that you have training and/or experience in that field. Some authors also send a picture of themselves but that is not necessary.

IV. MARKET POTENTIAL

Research the demographics and statistics of potential readers. For example: "The number of women living with children whose father was absent was over 10 million in 2002." This number will be significant if your book is about how a mother who is rearing her children alone can help them feel secure, excel in school, and make positive choices. These single mothers are all potential readers.

If your book were about motorcycles, you would want to have statistics on how many people own motorcycles. You would also want to tell how many motorcycle clubs, dealers, and accessory stores there are. Their club members and customers are potential readers, and your book could be sold through their club, store, or dealership.

Here's an example from a book proposal that attracted a publisher who subsequently published the book. The book, *Code to Victory: The Fact and Fiction of "Y" Intelligence,* by Arnold C. Franco and Paula Aselin Spellman, was a memoir of an Air Force veteran of World War II. The research turned up a large number of organizations whose members were potential buyers of this book. The following is a list of some of them.

> The American Legion; 3.1 million members
> The American Legion Auxiliary; 1 million members
> The Air Force Association; 180,000 members
> American Veterans of WWII, Korea & Vietnam (AMVETS);
>   200,000 members
> Veterans of Foreign Wars; 2,850,000 members
> The 9th Air Force Association; 2,500 members

In addition to the usual bookstore, Internet, and mail-order outlets, this book probably would sell well in PXs, officers' clubs, military-base gift shops, and at meetings, conventions, and events presented each year by many military organizations. It would very likely get reviewed in military publications and be carried in military and historical libraries.

For my own first book, *A Woman's Way: The Stop Smoking Book for Women,* I did a lot of my research in hospital libraries and, among other important facts, found out how many American women are smoking, what percentage of them want to quit, the health statistics for female versus male smokers, and the health effects on the fetuses, infants, and children of women smokers.

In addition to bookstores, other outlets for this book were women's clinics, gynecologists' offices, public health centers, and hospitals. Each facility ordered multiple copies of *A Woman's Way* for doctors, nurses, and therapists to give to their patients who smoked.

Debbie Puente, author of *Elegantly Easy Crème Brûlée and Other Custard Desserts*, discovered after her book was published that she could sell quite a few books doing book signings in gourmet markets, cookware shops, and other specialty stores. That kind of promotion virtually guarantees that those stores will carry the book.

Jean Wade, who wrote *How Sweet It Is . . . Without the Sugar,* a dessert cookbook for diabetics and people on low-sugar diets, was delighted to learn that her publisher sent her book for review to various magazines and periodicals dealing with health. Book reviews in major publications are even better than ads. In addition to bookstores, she does book signings in grocery stores that subsequently stock her books at their checkout stands.

After an excellent review in *CHOICE: Current Reviews for Academic Libraries,* meteorologist Stephen E. Blewett's book *What's in the Air: Natural and Man-Made Air Pollution* began selling steadily to public libraries and schools. It became a required textbook in several classes.

Knowing the possible outlets for your book at the time you are preparing your book proposal gives you a distinct advantage. Don't assume that the publisher will know how and where to market your book. You may have ideas the publisher hasn't even thought of.

V. COMPETITIVE WORKS

Research other books on the same subject. They are your competition. Borrow or buy books that may be similar to yours and read them. Choose four or five and list each by title, author, publisher, the year published, the number of pages, and the price. Write a brief synopsis of each one and explain how yours is different. Here's an example:

Codebreakers: The Inside Story of Bletchley Park; F. H. Hinsley and Alan Stripp, eds.; Oxford University Press; October 1994; paperback; illustrated; 321 pages; $14.95.

Bletchley Park, the top secret workplace of the cryptanalysts who cracked Germany's Enigma Code, is considered by some World War II historians to be the most successful intelligence operation in world history. This book is closest to Arnold Franco's as it deals with breaking the code of the Germans during World War II. It gives twenty-seven firsthand accounts written by the British and American members of the codebreakers' team.

The above book differs in significant ways from ***Code to Victory***, which is a personal memoir of author Franco who served as a cryptanalyst in a mobile unit that was to function with the advancing armies. His book also recalls the stories of others in his unit but, rather than being a compilation of stories, it is Franco's first-person account that includes the experiences of others in his unit.

Be sure the books you list are recent. Very old books will not be considered comparable.

VI. CHAPTER OUTLINE

Prepare a table of contents with chapter titles but without page numbers. Under each chapter title write a paragraph or two explaining what it is about. This indicates that you have a clear grasp of your subject and have planned exactly how and in what order you will present your information. Here's an example from my book proposal:

Chapter 1: A Cigarette Is NOT a Friend

Women often think of a cigarette as a friend, something that is always there when they are nervous, emotionally upset, lonely, or even celebrating. Smoking is a different addiction in women than it is in men. It is more damaging to their health and it's harder for them to quit.

Chapter 2: Pregnancy, PMS and Menopause

This chapter explains the danger to the fetus of a pregnant woman. It also tells how smoking can intensify premenstrual tension, and the increased tension, like a vicious cycle, makes it harder for women to quit. There is evidence that smoking can also bring on an early menopause.

VII. LIST OF ILLUSTRATIONS

If you have photographs, drawings, graphs, charts, maps, or other illustrations that will become a part of this work, list and describe each one. Also include samples.

SAMPLE CHAPTERS

You will be sending between one and three completed chapters, depending on what the publisher asks for. Always send the first chapter, because publishers usually want to know how you get into your subject. The first ten pages of your book are crucial. Actually, the first page is crucial, even the first few lines. You must grab the reader's interest right away. Here are some lines from the first pages of best-selling and/or classic novels:

My father has asked me to be the fourth corner at the Joy Luck Club. I am to replace my mother, whose seat at the mah jong table has been empty since she died two months ago. My father thinks she was killed by her own thoughts.
—*THE JOY LUCK CLUB*, BY AMY TAN

His two girls are curled together like animals whose habit is to sleep underground, in the smallest space possible.
—*ANIMAL DREAMS*, BY BARBARA KINGSOLVER

The large ballroom was crowded with familiar ghosts come to help celebrate her birthday. Kate Blackwell watched them mingle with the flesh-and-blood people, and in her mind, the scene was a dreamlike fantasy as the visitors from another time and place glided around the dance floor with the unsuspecting guests in black tie and long, shimmering evening gowns.

—*Master of the Game*, by Sidney Sheldon

It is a truth universally acknowledged that a single man in possession of a good fortune must be in want of a wife.

—*Pride and Prejudice*, by Jane Austen

And these are from best-selling nonfiction books (memoirs):

My father and mother should have stayed in New York where they met and married and where I was born. . . . When I look back on my childhood I wonder how I survived at all.

—*Angela's Ashes*, by Frank McCourt

As a boy, I never knew where my mother was from—where she was born, who her parents were. When I asked she'd say, "God made me." When I asked if she was white, she'd say, "I'm light-skinned," and change the subject. She raised twelve black children and sent us all to college . . ."

—*The Color of Water: A Black Man's Tribute to His White Mother*, by James McBride

The most famous first line of all time is, "It was the best of times, it was the worst of times," from the classic *A Tale of Two Cities* by Charles Dickens. That line drew you in and set the tone for the entire book.

The other two chapters you submit should be the ones you believe are the most important or most interesting. If you have a dynamite closing chapter, include it. Don't worry about giving away the ending. Your goal is to sell your book.

Book Proposal Checklist

Before you send your book proposal off to the publisher, double-check that you have done the following:

❏ Included a cover letter addressed to the person who requested the proposal, stating what you are sending and why

❏ Checked the spelling of the editor's name, company name, and address

❏ Proofread all of the material you are planning to send

❏ Included any additional material such as illustrations and everything else that was requested

❏ Made the margins at least one inch wide on the cover letter and all pages of the proposal

❏ Included your name, address, telephone and fax numbers, and e-mail address in the letter

❏ Signed your cover letter

❏ Included the title of your book on each page of the proposal

❏ Affixed the appropriate postage on the package

❏ Enclosed a stamped self-addressed envelope for a response and/or return of the proposal

Chapter 12

The Query Letter

Three questions are essential to all just criticism: What is the author's object? How far has he accomplished it? How far is that object worthy of approbation?
—NATHANIEL PARKER WILLIS

The query letter is usually one page long and single-spaced. If you absolutely cannot include all of the information on one page, go to a second page. The margins must be at least one inch wide on the sides and three-quarters of an inch at the bottom.

A query letter is a greatly condensed version of a book proposal. If your book is nonfiction, it is always a good idea to write your book proposal and a few chapters before sending out query letters. Publishers of novels usually want to see the entire manuscript, not just a book proposal. There are exceptions but they are rare. Preparing a proposal first will help you compose your query and, if an agent or publisher is interested in your idea and asks for more, you will be ready.

The information you will need to include in the query letter is virtually the same whether you are seeking an agent or a publisher. If you are sending the query directly to a publisher, simply change it accordingly. Instead of asking for representation, ask if they would be interested in publishing your book. Again, tailor your letter to the particular publisher you are contacting, being sure that they publish the kind of book you are writing.

HOW TO CHOOSE A PUBLISHER

In the chapter on agents I made suggestions on how to find the right agent for your book. However, you may choose to query a publisher directly and need to know which ones publish your kind of book. *Writer's Market* and *The Writer's Handbook* have that information but there are so many publishers listed that it will be very time-consuming to examine them all. You could also go to the library and look in *Literary Market Place* to check the type-of-publication and the subject indexes. One shortcut to choosing the right publisher for your book is to go to a bookstore and look in the section that has the kinds of books you are writing. Notice the titles that catch your eye. Pick up those books and briefly study them. Read the chapter titles on the contents page of nonfiction books. Read the first page of novels. When you find a book that has something in common with yours, write down the title, author, publishing company, and the year the book was published. You could also do this kind of research on Amazon.com. Often Amazon has sample pages that you can read online. Study best-seller lists, too, because the publishers of those books are probably doing a good job of promoting their books. If you find a book on that list that is in the same genre as yours, you will want to contact the publisher of it.

Then check those publishers' listings in the above-mentioned directories. There you will find out whether they want a query letter first or if they will accept a book proposal on first contact. You will learn where to send your letter and whom to address it to. Many publishers now have a Web site that you can go to in order to find out more about them. Often they will have their books listed, with brief synopses of them. Spend whatever time it takes to learn about publishing companies, including what kinds of books they publish, what they are looking for, if they want to see an outline, sample chapters, photos, or anything else and, most important of all, whether they accept submissions from authors. Major publishing houses such as Random House, Simon & Schuster, Harcourt, and HarperCollins, only accept agented submissions. It is a waste of your time and money to send queries or book proposals to publishers who refuse to look at manuscripts that have not been submitted by agents. Even though these publishers are listed in *Writer's Market,* you would not choose them unless you have some other way of getting their attention, such as knowing someone on the inside who will clear a path for you.

Many publishers now accept submissions by e-mail. If they list an e-mail address, you may contact them through the Internet asking whom you should send your query letter to and whether they would also like to see sample chapters, synopses, etc. It's always a good idea to find out who the current acquisitions editor is. The person whose name is listed in the directories may have left the company since the book was published. When you address your letter, check and double-check the spelling of the editor's name to be sure that it is accurate. I have heard of editors who throw the query letters into the trash if their name is misspelled. You'll have a better chance of getting his attention if you start off on the right foot.

Sometimes you can send both your query and any additional material that publishers want to see as an e-mail with attachments. It saves on paper, postage, and time to do it that way. Proofread everything you send, whether by e-mail or through the postal service. Even a brief note sent by e-mail should have proper spelling, punctuation, sentence structure, and grammar. People often get sloppy when they send e-mail. That may be fine when you are writing your friends or family, but when you are contacting an agent or publisher, you should be professional. You will be judged by what and how you write.

When you write your query letter, imagine what the literary agent or publisher's acquisitions editor who will be reading it will want to know, and answer the following questions.

- **What do you want?** Explain your purpose for writing: you have a manuscript on (subject matter) and you are seeking agency representation or a book publisher. The first paragraph should also include your "hook."
- **Why have you chosen this agency or publishing company?** Show that you have done your research by stating your reasons

for choosing that particular agent: author recommendation, the agent's reputation, the agent's track record of representing similar works, etc. If you are sending this to a publisher, mention that they have published similar types of books. If there is one that your book compares to in some way (for example, a historical novel, biography, how-to, or children's book) name the title and explain the similarities and differences.

- **What is your book about?** State the title and describe your book in a brief synopsis. This should not take up more than two or three lines. Read book jackets and ads for ideas.
- **What is your background?** Explain your qualifications for writing this book. Are you an expert in this particular field? List your other published works. If this is your first book, what else have you written? Television or film scripts? Magazine articles? Scientific papers?
- **What was your reason for writing this book?** Explain whether it is new information on the subject, a unique approach, or an unusual story. Tell why you wanted to write it.
- **Who will want to read it?** Target your audience so that a publisher will know how to market your book. Research is imperative here.
- **What do you have to show me?** Explain what you would like to send. If you have written a nonfiction book, ask if you may send a book proposal. If it is a novel, offer to send a synopsis of it or the full manuscript.

Your query letter should be concise, so choose your words carefully and check for spelling, grammatical construction, etc. This is the first example of your writing the agent or publisher will see, so make it the best it can be. Maintain a positive attitude about your creative work. Don't be apologetic or defensive. And if you want a reply one way or the other, *always send a self-addressed stamped envelope.*

Try to keep your query letter short. I have heard of three- and four-page query letters that got the attention of a publisher but they are exceptions to the rule.

Here are some examples to follow as you write your query letter.

THE FIRST PARAGRAPH

It's always a good idea to begin your letter with your "hook." Make your opening paragraph as powerful as you can. Include the title of your book in this paragraph. This is the most important part of your letter, so make sure it's a grabber. Here are two examples:

> One of the most baffling murder cases of the century began on a hot August night in Malibu with the brutal slaying of a beautiful porno star in the bedroom of noted TV evangelist Randy Saint. In *Saint and Sinner* I dissect the sloppy investigative work of the prosecution that put the wrong man on death row.

> Since ancient times, healers have told us our minds and bodies are one. Now, some amazing new research has proven this connection. A number of highly respected scientists and physicians have documented "miracle" cures using the power of the mind. This instant healing is something everyone can do and in my book, *If You Can Love, You Can Heal,* I explain how.

THE BODY OF THE LETTER

Briefly synopsize your book. Include in the description of your book some of the more interesting passages, unknown facts, or your own involvement in the story, if pertinent. Here are two examples:

> Smoking is not the same addiction in women as it is in men. By the year 2000, women's death rate from smoking surpassed men's. This book addresses those differences and shows women how they can quit for good—without gaining weight. Because my own mother died prematurely from the effects of years of smoking, this book is dedicated to her.

> Born into wealth on a cotton plantation in the Old South sixteen years before the start of the Civil War, Susanna Campbell was given everything she could ever want except her parent's love. The delicate and beautiful girl was closer to her

black nanny than she was to her own family. Still, no one could have predicted that Susanna would spend the Civil War years risking her life hiding runaway slaves. This true story is told through her recently discovered journals.

Explain your reasons for writing the book and tell a little about yourself.

As a physical therapist with a master's degree in psychology, I have found that the most valuable help for a child recovering from a serious accident is a therapeutic process I developed after my own devastating accident. Using this procedure, children get well in half the usual time.

Tell what the market for the book is and, in the last paragraph, describe what you would like to send. For help in writing the query letter go to your book proposal and highlight the most important points.

The Closing Paragraph

Describe what you would like to send. Your research may have indicated whether the agent or publisher would like to see the whole manuscript, a book proposal, or a synopsis. If it is a book proposal, explain briefly what it consists of. Example:

I would like to send you my book proposal along with three sample chapters, a total of sixty-five pages.

Query Letter Checklist

Before you send off your letter, look over this checklist to be sure you have done the following:

❑ Gotten the name of the current acquisitions editor
❑ Checked the spelling of the editor's name, company name, and address
❑ Proofread the query letter and all other material you are planning to send

❑ Made the margins at least one inch wide
❑ Included your name, address, telephone and fax numbers, and e-mail address in the letter
❑ Made a compelling statement and included the title of your book in the first paragraph
❑ Given your experience, credentials, and/or reason for writing the book
❑ Described your book
❑ Stated who the intended audience is and, if known, how to reach it
❑ Stated in the last paragraph what action you are asking for
❑ Signed your letter
❑ Affixed the appropriate postage on the envelope or package
❑ Enclosed a stamped self-addressed envelope for a response

Chapter 13

The Literary Agency Agreement

A verbal agreement isn't worth the paper it's written on.
—ATTRIBUTED TO SAMUEL GOLDWYN

Any written agreement can be a legally enforceable contract. The following information should not be construed as legal advice, merely a discussion of what to expect in agreements you make with an agent, publisher, or collaborator, and what to watch out for. Because laws and procedures are different in different states, countries, and industries, and are subject to change, you are advised to get qualified legal advice before signing any agreement. Sometimes authors are so excited about finding an agent or a publisher who is interested in their book that they will sign just about anything. Remember the old saying, "Act in haste, repent at leisure," and proceed with caution.

In chapter 10 the role of the agent was explained. Once you have found an agent who you think is the right one to represent you and your works, and that agent has offered you representation, there are a number of questions you should ask.

The Association of Authors' Representatives (AAR) has a list of twenty-two topics they suggest you discuss. Until you know more about the agency, it is not advisable to sign any contracts.

Find out if the agent is a member of the Association of Author's Representatives. All members must abide by a Canon of Ethics and satisfy the requirements for AAR membership, which includes experience in the field. To qualify for membership the agent must have been "principally responsible for executed agreements concerning the grant of publication, translation or performance rights in ten different literary properties during the eighteen-month period preceding application." Here are some other questions to ask.

- How long has your agency been in business and how many people are employed in the agency?
- Who in the agency will actually be handling my work?
- Will that person keep me apprised of the work the agency is doing on my behalf?
- Will you provide editorial input and career guidance?
- Do you provide submission lists and copies of publishers' rejection letters?
- Will you consult with me on all offers?
- What is your commission? (Most charge 15 percent for basic sales to U.S. publishers.)
- How do you process and disburse client funds?
- Do you charge for expenses incurred in handling my work, such as postage, phone charges, and copying costs and, if so, will you itemize such expenses for me?
- Do you issue annual 1099 tax forms?
- What do you expect of me as your client?

Taking the time to discuss those matters will help smooth the relationship with your agent. Before getting involved you must know what the agent's responsibility is and what yours is. One complaint agents make is that their clients expect them to be available to speak with them at all times. They also grumble that authors think agents aren't doing their job if they don't get them a deal with a publisher. But, the agents say, some manuscripts just aren't marketable for any number of reasons and they have so many clients that they can't talk to each one every day on the phone. They need time to contact publishers. That's in the best interest of the client.

Many writers say that after they signed the agreement with their agent they never heard from him again. The agent wouldn't even return their phone calls. Writers are often disappointed that their agent did not take an interest in their writing career.

Even if you feel that everything you wanted to know was addressed, other questions will come up during the course of your agent-author relationship, and maintaining clear and friendly lines of communication will make it easier on both of you.

For a small fee the AAR will furnish you with a list of their members. Agents are listed according to their specialization: L = Literary, D = Dramatic, and C = Children. They will not make recommendations to authors seeking representation, though.

Not all agents supply an agreement or contract for you to sign. Often the agent and author agree to terms informally. It's always a good idea to have the terms spelled out in a memo or letter from your agent. If the agent does not prepare an agreement, you can write one, based upon your understanding of the relationship, and send it to the agent asking if you are correct in your assumptions. That way there are likely to be fewer misunderstandings.

If you are offered a contract, discuss anything that is unclear to you with the agent and be sure that you understand it before you sign. Get as much information as you can before you sign any agreement with an agent (or anyone, for that matter). There is a great deal of valuable contract information in *The Writer's Legal Guide,* Third Edition, by Tad Crawford and Kay Murray, and in *Business and Legal Forms for Authors and Self-Publishers* by Tad Crawford. Another good resource is *The Writer's Legal Companion: The Complete Handbook for the Working Writer* by Brad Bunnin and Peter Beren. It covers agency and publishing contracts, protecting your copyright, libel, taxes, and much more. The authors offer suggestions as to what issues should be covered in an agency contract. They go into these issues in greater detail in their book but here is a brief discussion of them.

THE GRANT OF AUTHORITY

Set limits on your agent's authority to act in your behalf. You should have ultimate control over the sale of your rights. Agents should not have the power to sign a contract and bind you to it.

THE AGENT'S OBLIGATION

What will your agent do for you? This should be spelled out clearly. The agent should use her "best efforts" to sell your work and to act in "good faith" on your behalf. She should make a conscientious effort to sell your work. She should submit *all* offers to you, whether or not she thinks you should accept any of them. The agent should keep in touch with you and return your phone calls. You can't expect a busy, active agent to spend hours on the phone with you. But if you have not heard from her for a few months, it's reasonable to think she's forgotten you, and a call to her would be in order.

The deals you make and the contracts you sign are your own personal business, and your agent should keep your financial affairs private and confidential. It is unethical for your agent to brag about the deal she got for you or the advance you received. Such loose talk could jeopardize future dealings with publishers.

Your agent should counsel and advise you, giving you the benefit of her experience. If she doesn't take the time to explain to you why you should or should not accept a particular offer, she isn't doing her job.

As the relationship between the agent and author can become an intensely personal one, you may want to be sure that the agency will not arbitrarily assign you to another agent in the future. Employees come and go, and if the agent with whom you have established rapport leaves the agency, you may wish to terminate your relationship with the agency. Will the agency ask your permission before transferring you to someone else? This is a matter that should be clarified at the time you sign the agreement.

THE AUTHOR'S OBLIGATION

Your obligation is to pay a commission when your agent sells your work. You may decide you want an exclusive agency relationship wherein you would not owe the agent a commission if you sold the work yourself. This might be the best kind of arrangement for you if you have extensive contacts within the publishing industry and have reason to believe that you could very well make a deal with a publisher on the golf course. (And probably more deals are made there than are made in offices.) Under this type of agreement, however, you must compensate your agent if *another* agent gets the deal for you. In that case, you would owe commissions to both agents.

Most agents want an exclusive sale agreement, where you would be obligated to pay a commission no matter who sold your work. For most new authors that is probably okay. But beware of any arrangement where you end up selling your future.

Make sure your agent is representing you for a particular property or for specific works. In no case should you agree to let him represent everything you have ever written or will write in the future.

WARRANTIES

Both you and your agent need to warrant that you are free to enter the agreement, that you will be able to fully perform your obligation, and that you do not have any other contracts that will conflict with the provisions of the agency agreement.

Just as writers can tell horror stories about their agents, agents have some hair-raising tales about their clients. They've had clients who plagiarized someone else's work and represented it as their own, or who sold their work themselves without notifying them.

COMMISSIONS

Literary agents whose main client base consists of authors of books usually charge 15 percent. Agents who represent film or television writers generally charge a 10 percent commission. The Writers Guild of America (WGA) maintains a list of signatory agents who represent material such as screenplays, teleplays, stories, treatments, plot outlines, formats, breakdowns, sketches, and narrations. Here is an excerpt from the WGA Agreement with Agents:

> The Guild disapproves of the practice followed by certain agencies of charging a "reading fee" or some similar fee to writers who submit literary material to them. Accordingly, the

Guild will not be willing to list any such agency. The only monies listed agencies may collect from their clients is a 10 percent commission after successfully negotiating a deal.

As the author of a manuscript for a book, you would not ordinarily go to a WGA agent. Some exceptions might be made if you have written a novel that would translate well onto the screen or a nonfiction book that could be made into a film or TV documentary. But even then, most experienced writers and agents will tell you that your best chance of getting it produced is to get it published as a book first.

As this is about getting your book completed and published, you will be seeking a literary agent who represents authors, not scriptwriters. There is no guild that tells those agents what they must charge. The fee is negotiable, however, and if you have extensive contacts and can help your agent get a publishing deal, you may be able to negotiate a 10 percent commission. For foreign sales the commission ranges up to 20 percent. That is because the agent often has to split the commission with an agent in another country.

Your agent may also ask for an advance of about $100 for some out-of-pocket expenses such as postage, long-distance calling, and photocopying. That is not an unreasonable request and most agents will give you an accounting of how the money was spent.

The agency agreement usually provides for the publisher to pay your royalties directly to the agent, who takes his percentage out and writes a check to you for the balance. As your agent will likely be able to read and understand a royalty statement better than you, that puts him in the position of monitoring the publisher.

Three things that should definitely be in the written agreement are (1) that your agent pays you your share promptly, (2) that you are allowed to examine the account books at any time, and (3) that your money is kept in a client trust account, separate from the agency's own funds.

MULTIPLE AGENTS

As your agent may not be able to represent you for film and television sales, you may wish to sign with a WGA-approved agent in addition to your literary agent. You are not required to grant any one agent the authority over your entire bundle of rights. You can have different types of agents representing your different types of rights. You will need to specify the type of work the agent will be representing and be sure that you are not giving the agent any later works you may produce or for which you already have an established market. You may want the agent to represent your book but not your magazine articles or scripts.

THE CONTRACT TERM

You may want to give your agent a definite amount of time to represent you. Usually one year is sufficient to find out whether the agent can sell your work, whether you are compatible, and whether you trust him enough to want to continue to work with him.

An agent may want more time because it may take many years before an author begins to earn significant income from her writing. If you still feel comfortable with your agent after a year, even if he hasn't made a deal, you may want to stay with him.

TERMINATING THE AGREEMENT

You may not want to commit to a year or to any definite period of time. You may want the freedom to terminate the relationship at any time after giving a thirty-day notice. Then, if it doesn't seem to be working out, you can move on to another agent.

Some agency agreements contain post-termination clauses stating that they are owed a commission if you or another agent sells your work to a publisher within ninety days after termination of the agreement. If your agent has been working hard trying to sell your manuscript and has made a number of impressive contacts, that's a reasonable and fair request.

LEARNING MORE

Whenever possible, before you sign an agreement for representation, speak to an author the agent has represented and ask whether there were any problems with that agent. The American Society of Journalists and Authors, the National Writers Association, and the National Writers Union maintain files on agents their members have worked with.

The NWU has a Preferred Literary Agent Agreement and a guide, "Understanding the Author-Agent Relationship," that are available to members. Their guide is an educational tool to help you understand and evaluate your agreement. It explains that an author's work is a bundle of individual rights including hardcover print rights, paperback print rights, electronic database rights, interactive software rights, foreign translation rights, television adaptation rights, and audio cassette rights, to name a few. Collectively, they form the copyright to the author's work. The author owns these rights until she signs them away. Each right may be licensed or transferred independently of the others. The NWU explains, "this principle is known as the 'Doctrine of Divisibility' and is a cornerstone of U.S. copyright law."

Agent agreements should be "work-specific" advises the NWU. Be wary of any agreement that gives the agent automatic authority to represent future works that you may produce for a publisher. The agent's authority should be clearly defined in the original contract.

Agents sometimes offer "work-for-hire" agreements in which the author gives up the copyright of her own creation. Work-for-hire and all-rights agreements may indicate that the agent is not really an agent but a packager.

Also beware if an agent represents both parties in a collaboration agreement. That raises the potential for a conflict of interest.

Whatever agreement you make with your agent, be sure that you both understand it completely and that the details are in writing.

Chapter 14

The Publishing Agreement

*Book publishing is in the midst of an authentic revolution
. . . and the book contract is changing so fast that one
simply cannot speak meaningfully of a "standard" book
deal.*

—Jonathan Kirsch,
Kirsch's Guide to the Book Contract

Many changes have taken place in the publishing world over the past few years, which have made the publishing contract more complex than ever. As I am not a lawyer, I cannot give you legal advice, but I can alert you to some of the elements to consider.

Technology is the major reason for the ever-changing publishing contract. The twentieth century brought with it many new and different ways to record and transmit written works. Along with audiotape and videotape machines came radio, film, and television. Following on the heels of photocopying machines were personal computers, scanners, and printers. The computer made the Internet possible and that development made copyrighted material available to everyone on a massive scale. This explosion of new technologies has presented the enormous challenge of defining and protecting authors' rights to their literary creations.

Among the rights that must be spelled out in a publishing contract are paperback rights, book club rights, photocopying and facsimile rights, microfilm rights, audio rights, motion picture and television rights, and the various categories of electronic rights that are evolving so fast that they defy legal definitions.

All of this makes a chapter on publishing contracts impossible to write in a comprehensive way. As media, technologies, and markets change, a contract that works today is out of date tomorrow.

What you will see here is an overview that should help familiarize you with the kinds of agreements that have been used.

Before you sign any agreement with a publisher, be sure you know what you are signing. If you have an active, qualified agent with current contacts in the publishing field, she can help you understand the details of your contract. If you do not have an agent, it would be wise to get some legal advice from an attorney who specializes in, or at least is familiar with, publishing law. If neither of those options is available to you, get a recently published book that contains information on publishers' contracts. There are probably a number of good books on the subject but those mentioned in the preceding chapter are some that I can recommend. *Business and Legal Forms for Authors and Self-Publishers* by Tad Crawford contains a standard book publishing contract. It also explains the fine points of the contract including the grant of rights, compensation, artistic control, and more. A negotiation checklist is included to help you understand and negotiate your agreement.

You can't expect to find a model contract that will cover every situation. As Jonathan Kirsch says, "the book contract is a moving target." Each agreement must be fine-tuned to suit the author, the publisher, and the project.

Two publications by the National Writers Union are very informative and would be helpful to authors. They are *NWU Guide to Book Contracts* and *NWU Guide to Fair Use*. Both are available through the National Writers Union.

Here are some things to look for in a book contract.

GRANT OF RIGHTS

"Primary rights" will include hardcover, trade paperback, mass-market paperback, translation, periodical publication, book club, photocopying and facsimile, microfilm, general print publication, direct-response marketing, sound recordings, electronic books, publishing-on-demand, database, networks, and online services, interactive and multimedia rights.

Each of these items needs to be considered carefully and designed to fit your specific needs and wants. For example, if you have written a how-to book such as this, you might want to negotiate the right to sell your book at seminars you are presenting. In that case, you might be able to purchase books from the publisher at a discount and sell the books at full retail price. You may want to sell your books directly to the consumer, especially if you have an extensive mailing list of people who you know will be interested in your book.

"Secondary rights" are dramatic, reading, motion picture and television, radio, commercial, and future media and technologies rights.

Those are called the "bundle of rights" that make up the most fundamental *deal points* in a book contract. *Deal points* as used here means the points considered essential to the parties making a book deal and include rights, territory, term, advance, and royalties.

"Electronic rights" is a term that can have many meanings with the proliferation of new technologies. It is particularly challenging because things are changing too fast for settled legal definitions. There are no "standard" electronic rights clauses in publishing contracts. Be sure this is addressed in very specific language in your contract. It should be spelled out clearly who owns the right to exploit a book through a "publishing-on-demand" system, for example. Also called "print-on-demand," these computer-based systems are changing the way books are distributed and sold. In some areas the system is in place whereby a bookstore customer can order an "e-book" from a catalog. The book can then be printed out from an electronic database, bound, and delivered on the spot.

AUTHOR COMPENSATION

"Advance against royalties" is money the author gets before the book is published. Often it is paid at the rate of one-third upon signing the agreement, one-third upon delivery of an acceptable manuscript, and one-third upon publication of the book. That money is not a no-strings gift from the publisher. It is deducted from future royalties on the sale of the book. Thus an author may not receive any royalty checks for a year or more.

How important is an advance? It depends on a number of factors. If an advance will allow you the freedom to work on your book instead of working a full-time job, it could be very important. Also, if you receive a significant advance, the publisher will want to protect its investment by advertising and promoting your book more aggressively.

"Royalties on publisher's editions" is the share of sales the author receives. In the past this was often a percentage of the retail or cover price of the book. For example, if the price printed on the book cover was $10 and the author's royalty rate was 10 percent, the author received a dollar for each copy sold. A more frequent arrangement now is for the percentage to be based on the "invoice price," which is what the publisher receives from bookstores and wholesalers. Because a publisher may give them a discount of 40 percent or more, the publisher's net on a $10 book might be $6, in which case the author would receive 60 cents per book.

THE MANUSCRIPT

"Delivery of manuscript" has to do with the date and form in which the author has agreed to deliver the completed manuscript. The publisher may ask for a computer disk containing the manuscript in a word-processing program, and a hard copy (a printout).

"Artwork, permissions, index, and other materials" may include original art, illustrations, photos, charts, an index, bibliography, contents page, introduction, etc. It may also involve authorizations, permissions, and endorsements.

"Publisher's rights on delivery" allows the publisher to terminate the agreement without further obligation to the author if the publisher finds the manuscript or any of the materials unacceptable. The publisher may give the author the opportunity to make revisions or corrections and resubmit. This clause also gives the publisher the right to terminate the agreement if the material is not delivered on time. In this case, the author will probably be required to repay the publisher for any advance she has received. The publisher may terminate the contract if changed outside conditions, such as world events, have adversely affected the salability of the work but, in that event, the author is usually allowed to keep the advance.

PUBLICATION

This section deals with authorizing the publisher to edit and revise the work, to design the book, set the price, print, advertise, and promote it, among other things. It may also provide for revisions and state the date of publication and the number of free copies the author will receive.

COPYRIGHT

This states that the publisher shall apply for a copyright in the name of the author and place the notice in the book. It also has to do with possible copyright infringement and how the parties may handle litigation.

ACCOUNTING

The publisher sets up a formal system of accounting where it credits the author's account with royalties and any other payments, and debits it for the advance, returned books, etc. This also states the author's audit rights.

AGENCY

The author authorizes and appoints the agent to act on behalf of the author to collect and receive payments and other communications from the publisher.

WARRANTIES, REPRESENTATIONS, AND INDEMNITIES

The author is asked to guarantee that his work will not result in a lawsuit and agrees to bear all costs of defending a claim if one is made. The author warrants that the work is not in public domain because, if anyone can freely publish it, the publisher doesn't have to acquire the rights from the author in the first place. The author also states that he is the sole proprietor of the work and has the authority to enter the agreement and grant the rights.

It is your job, as an author, to protect your rights. You can't expect anyone else to do that for you. That is why you must educate yourself about copyrights, literary agents, book publishers, and each and every contract and agreement you may be asked to sign.

Chapter 15

The Collaboration Agreement

The first issue to be resolved is how the copyright in the collaboration will be owned.

—TAD CRAWFORD,
BUSINESS AND LEGAL FORMS FOR AUTHORS AND SELF-PUBLISHERS

Will you be collaborating with someone else on a book? Have you been asked to ghostwrite a book? Are you a person with ideas who is looking for an experienced writer to get your thoughts down on paper? There are many different kinds of collaborations, and the agreements must be in writing if you are to avoid some really sticky problems later on. In every case the details of the agreement should be spelled out. For example, the names of the parties and the names of their agents, if any, should be stated. The nature or subject of the work must be specified, such as autobiography, how-to book, child psychology, cookbook, etc. The tentative or working title should be named, and if there is an outline or synopsis of the work, it should be attached to the contract.

GHOSTWRITING

A ghostwriter is one who writes for and gives credit of authorship to another person. If you are hired to help a person write his autobiography, you may be hired as a ghostwriter. Sometimes specialists in certain fields will hire a ghostwriter to explain esoteric concepts in a way that the lay public will understand. Whether you are hired to ghostwrite or will be contracting with a writer to ghostwrite your book, you need to know all the ramifications.

Before a contract is even considered, both parties should decide on two major issues: the charges and the author credit. *Writer's Market* contains guidelines in these matters. They list "Ghostwriting, as told to" which is writing for a celebrity or expert, and "Ghostwriting, no credit" which could be writing for an individual who is self-publishing, or for a book packager, publisher, agent, or company.

The ghostwriter of the former (as told to) receives a "with" credit line: *John Q. Public with Jane Doe.* This appears on the cover of the book. If a book publisher is involved, a typical deal might be that the ghost gets the full advance plus 50 percent of royalties. Self-publishers might pay an hourly rate to the writer, which could range from $25 to $85, or pay by the page at a rate of $125 to $175 per book page.

A person ghostwriting with no credit could expect a rate of anywhere from a low of $5,000 to a high of $50,000 or more per title, plus expenses. The ghost who is working for a self-publisher should ask for one-fourth down payment, one-fourth when the book is half finished, one-fourth at the three-quarters mark, and the balance upon completion. In any case, it is wise to charge extra for researching, because that can be very time-consuming.

In *Business and Legal Forms for Authors and Self-Publishers* (Allworth Press) attorney/author/publisher Tad Crawford notes, "It is important that the credits accurately reflect what the parties did. The credit could be 'by A and B' or 'story by A and illustrations by B.' 'As told to' indicates one person telling their story to another; while 'with' suggests that one person did some writing and the other person, usually a professional author, shaped and completed the book. It is against public policy for someone to take credit for writing a book which, in fact, was written by someone else."

EQUAL PARTNER COLLABORATIONS

If it is a joint work and proceeds are equally shared, either party can license the work; this should be outlined in the contract. Each party's responsibility should be set out in great detail as well as how they will authorize and share expenses. They also need to decide what will happen if the project is never completed. The issues might be what their individual rights will be in case the book project is never sold. Each author would probably want to retain the right to publish the portion of the book he wrote and be free to publish it by itself or include it in a longer work.

There are so many variables in any collaboration agreement that they can't all be addressed here. But think of all the contingencies you can and detail them in the contract. Some additional points to consider are:

- Specify a date by which time the work should be completed
- Make out a work schedule with sequential deadlines
- State whether the parties will self-publish if they do not receive a publishing contract
- Allow for termination of the contract and state the conditions
- Require that each partner receive a copy of the contract
- Specify which author's name goes first on the book
- Decide what will happen in the event of the death or disability of either party
- Discuss promotion, including the use of the parties' names, photos, and bios

More information on collaboration contracts, complete with a CD-ROM containing a form you can modify and print out, can be found in *Business and Legal Forms for Authors and Self-Publishers*. The National Writers Union also provides a guide and a Model Ghostwriting & Collaborations Contract to their members. See Resources in the back of this book for contact information.

OTHER CONTRACTS AND AGREEMENTS

Some agreements may be oral contracts where nothing is written down. However, even if your agreement is oral, it is always wise to write a "memo of understanding" where you simply spell out the agreement as you understand it and ask the other party to confirm that this was the way she understood it as well. As an editor and literary consultant, I have signed agreements provided by my clients, such as nondisclosure agreements. I always agree to that because it puts them at ease. When there were details I wanted to be sure my clients understood, I have prepared a memo of understanding and asked them to sign and date it, indicating that they were in agreement. These memos were mainly to clarify what I would be doing and what my charges would be. For the same project I might charge an hourly rate for some of the work, such as editing, and a flat rate for others, such as page design, news releases, and back-cover writing. It simply made it easier on all of us to keep track—and to keep *on track*—of how we had chosen to work with each other.

As an author, you may be called upon to sign a lecture contract, an agreement with an independent contractor, or a privacy release. You may need to get permissions from owners of copyrighted materials such as illustrations, photos, paintings, articles, poems, song lyrics, or quotations from books. There are forms for these concerns as well as many more in *Business and Legal Forms for Authors and Self-Publishers*, mentioned above.

Chapter 16

The Many Ways of Getting Published

*Books, like men their authors, have no more than one way
of coming into the world, but there are ten thousand to go
out of it, and return no more.*

—JONATHAN SWIFT, *A TALE OF A TUB*

Maybe in Swift's time there was only one way books came into
the world, but that has changed. You, the author, have many choices
now. There are more ways to get published than ever before. The
costs range from nothing if you sign a contract with an established
publisher to thousands of dollars if you choose to self-publish. Here
are a few of the ways your book might be published, with some pros
and cons of each one.

BEING PUBLISHED BY A TRADITIONAL BOOK PUBLISHER

Advantages: Not only will it cost you nothing, you probably will get an
advance. The publisher will pay for printing, editing, promotion, distribution, etc. The general perception among bookstores and book
buyers is that a book published by an established publisher is more
professional and of a higher quality than a self-published book.

Disadvantages: The author loses much of the control. Income from royalties could be less than the author's potential profit from a self-published book. It will take eighteen months to two years for the publisher to get the book out.

Selling your book to a publisher doesn't mean that you can just sit back and wait until the royalties start rolling in. You still have responsibilities. For more details on this, see chapter 17, Working with a Publisher.

BEING PUBLISHED BY AN E-BOOK (ELECTRONIC BOOK) PUBLISHER

Advantages: As an e-book publisher's costs are a great deal lower than those for a printed-book publisher, the author has a greater chance of getting accepted.

Disadvantages: This is still a fairly new and unproven field of publishing and finding a qualified e-book publisher is challenging.

As e-book publishing is an area I am not familiar with, I asked Virginia Lawrence, Ph.D., who owns Cognitext.com and is an expert in this field, for advice. She says that e-books are similar to printed books in that both depend on the talent of the writer as well as the quality of the marketing. "A narrow, well-defined group thirsting for knowledge is the perfect e-book target market," she explained. "There are success stories in e-book publishing. Those successes are built on outstanding marketing aimed at one specific portion of the reading market."

CO-PUBLISHING WITH AN ESTABLISHED PUBLISHER

Advantages: The publisher will know how to edit, promote, and distribute the book. The costs of producing the book will be shared. You will have the benefit of the publisher's professional input and advice.

Disadvantages: You will have less control than if you did it all yourself. You must share profits with the other publisher. There could be disagreements that are difficult to work out.

SELF-PUBLISHING A PRINTED BOOK

Advantages: As the quality of self-published books improves, the negative perception is changing. You, as both author and publisher, make all of the decisions and have control of the entire process. All profits belong to you alone. Once it is finished and typeset, you can get your book printed and bound within two weeks (with a digital short-run printer) to two months (with a traditional offset printer). If you have a niche market that you know you can sell to, you could make a greater profit publishing your own book this way than you could any other way.

Disadvantages: Printing costs can range from a few hundred dollars to $10,000 or more. If you are unable to do everything yourself to get your book ready for the printer, you must find qualified people to perform some of the services for you. They include editing, creating the cover and interior design, typesetting the book, and putting it into a portable document format (PDF) to send to the printer, all of which will be costly. You, as the publisher, are responsible for all the promotion, distribution, and sales. Unless you have a ready market for it, you may never recover your initial costs to produce the book. You may also end up with several hundred or more unsold books.

For more information on this kind of publishing, see chapter 18, Publishing Your Own Book.

There are ways to self-publish a book that do not require the services of a printing company or bindery. Following are a few ideas.

SELF-PUBLISHING A SPIRAL-BOUND BOOK

Advantages: Photocopies can be made and books bound the same day by most photocopying stores, such as Kinko's. You can purchase a binding machine and bind them yourself as you need them. You can also run off high-quality copies of the pages on your own laser printer. Many cookbooks are spiral bound because the pages lay flat, making it easier for the cook to follow the recipes.

Disadvantages: It can end up costing more than a digital short-run printing company would charge and may not look as professional. Spiral-bound books have no spine on which to put the title of the book and because of that, many bookstores and libraries will not carry them.

There are spiral-bound books where the cover is folded so that there is a spine. However, that process may not be available from a local photocopying company nor to an individual using a spiral binding machine.

CREATING A HAND-CRAFTED BOOK

Advantages: This may be appropriate for art books, poetry, or family history. It can become a work of art in itself or a family heirloom. It is a great creative outlet for authors who are also artists or craftsmen and who enjoy the process of creating the entire product. The author has total control. If the author chooses not to bind it himself, he can send it out to be hand-bound for $6 to $10 per book cover.

Disadvantages: Depending upon the materials used, it could be quite costly per unit. Only limited numbers of books could be produced this way. Handcrafting a book is a time-consuming process.

PRODUCING AN AUDIO BOOK

Advantages: You could record it yourself in a quiet room of your home or office, in which case the only costs would be the audiotape or compact discs. It can be "read" by the blind or listened to on long automobile trips. It can be produced in the author's own voice, which would be valuable for family histories and memoirs. Later it could be transcribed and made into a printed book.

Disadvantages: For good sound quality you would need to record it in a professional recording studio with a sound engineer, which could be expensive. Promotion and distribution would be challenging. If you don't have a pleasant voice that records well, you may have to hire a professional actor.

SELF-PUBLISHING AN E-BOOK

Advantages: You would save money on printing costs. All you would need are a computer, a word-processing program, and Adobe Acrobat to convert your book into a PDF (portable document format) file. E-books can be sold on floppy disks or CDs and you can make copies yourself. Disks and CDs are less bulky to carry than a printed book. They can be read on a computer screen or printed out.

Disadvantages: They are too easily copied. It would be hard to get bookstores to carry them. You would still have to find ways to promote your book, and sales of e-books have been disappointing.

This format is the most interesting one of all if you want to keep your costs down and become involved in a new technology in book publishing.

Chapter 17

Working with a Publisher

[A book] is not an article of mere consumption but fairly of capital, and often in the case of professional men, setting out in life, it is their only capital.

—THOMAS JEFFERSON

Once your book is accepted by a publisher, you become partners. You supply the materials, the publisher supplies the capital, and together you produce a product. Of course, it's not that cold or that simple. It is a business relationship, however. It is—or should be—a relationship of trust, cooperation, and mutual respect. You share a common goal, that of creating a high-quality, commercially viable product you both can be proud of.

Even when you realize that you are involved in a business partnership, it is hard to remove yourself emotionally from that book you created. If you are like most authors, your blood, sweat, tears, and a huge amount of your time went into the production of your manuscript. It is more than an inanimate object to you. It is part of your heart and mind. It may be hard to accept anyone changing that piece of yourself. Yet, you must.

There can also be misunderstandings between author and publisher because it is rare for someone else to see things exactly the way you see them. It will be easier to see the big picture when you know what to expect once you sign the publication agreement. You will find the process more enjoyable if you are able to accept the following.

- You are not your publisher's only author and possibly not even his favorite.
- You may have to make compromises that could tear at your heart.
- Some of your favorite passages may be taken out.
- You may be required to write a few more chapters.
- It will seem to take forever before your book appears in bookstores.
- You must be patient.

There are many things to consider and, although you may share your opinions with the publisher, he is the one who must make most of the decisions. He will be the one to choose the size of the book, whether to publish it in hard cover or paperback, and what to charge for it. But before it even gets to the point of printing and binding, it will go through many processes, and that takes time.

THE AUTHOR'S RESPONSIBILITY

It is of the utmost importance that you meet the publisher's deadlines. If you do not get all the necessary materials and information to him on time, it could delay the release date of your book.

Among your responsibilities are the following:

- To edit your work carefully, checking for punctuation, spelling, and grammatical errors.
- To be accurate, check your facts and, whenever possible, furnish your sources.
- To avoid any possibility of plagiarism or defamation of character in your writing. You could jeopardize not only your own reputation but your publisher's too.

- To be professional at all times. Keep your personal problems to yourself.
- To be fair and open-minded. Try to see the publisher's viewpoint.

You will probably be expected to provide both a printed copy and a CD or a disk of your manuscript. Most people now have computers and inkjet or laser printers. If you don't, you may have to get someone with a computer setup to put your manuscript into a Word file, print it out, and save it to a disk for sending to your publisher. Your publisher may ask you to use their "house style" in preparing your manuscript. If he doesn't, you could use the following guidelines furnished by Allworth Press. They are in accordance with the current industry standard.

Manuscript Style Guidelines for Authors

THE MANUSCRIPT

Please provide a file and a hard copy of the manuscript. It is preferable that the file is saved in a standard format (recent versions of Microsoft Word or WordPerfect, or as a rich text format [.rtf] file). If this is a difficulty, *please call to ensure that we will be able to read the files.*

The manuscript should be complete. Information, including bibliographic information and appendixes, should not be left incomplete, unless clearly marked on the pages. With regard to the formatting of the manuscript files, please note the following:

- If you are new to computers, please ask someone to show you how simple it is to use word wrap—that is, allowing the word processing program to wrap your words through to the next line without interruption. Do not use the computer as a typewriter and put carriage returns after each line.
- Manuscripts should be double-spaced with one-inch margins. Do not use condensed type or any special type-faces. We prefer that you use Times New Roman (or Times

or Times Roman), because these fonts seem to translate cross-platform fluidly (i.e., from your Mac to our PC; from our PC to the designer's page-layout software). Other fonts often cause proofreading nightmares due to translation problems (hyphens become = signs, quotes become capital As and @ marks, and so on).

- Justify text to the left margin only.
- The fewer commands on the disk, the better. In the running text, do not underline; do not bold (except for subheads); do not capitalize entire words.
- Do not skip a space between paragraphs.
- Do not put more than one space between sentences.
- Indent paragraphs.
- Do not indent the first paragraph of a chapter, subheads, or the first paragraph below a subhead; these should all be flush left.
- Use subheads, consistently indicating whether each subhead is *A* or *B*. *A* is a subhead and *B* is a sub-subhead. To indicate which is which, A-heads should be consistently flush left, and B-heads should be consistently indented. If you have C sub-sub-subheads, they should be indented and styled as 10 point, as opposed to 12 point, type. Use a subhead for each new subject. A subhead should occur about every two hundred words (roughly once per double-spaced page). If absolutely necessary, a C sub-sub-subhead can also be used, but is discouraged.
- Skip a space before subheads.
- Use the spell-check on all text.

USE OF IMAGES

If your book is going to contain illustrated materials (i.e. photographs, charts, graphs, and so on), you should let us know how many there are and where these items will need to be placed. We will accept images in multiple formats (digital, black-and-white prints, transparencies, etc.), but please let us know in advance what formats you plan to use. If you are using digital images, our printer has specifications as to file size, resolution, and type of file. Make sure that you number all images and that the number corresponds to

1. A numbered caption, if one is necessary
2. A place marker in the text

For example, if you are using slides in your book, you should number the slides 1, 2, 3, 4, etc. Then, in the text at the appropriate place you should insert the marker **[insert slide 1 here]**. When the typesetter goes through the file, he will be able to substitute the correct image for the correct place marker.

If you are using digital files, please make sure that the file name corresponds to the place marker in the text. If your file is called girl2.tif, make sure that the place marker in the file says **[insert girl2.tif]**.

It is extremely important that pictures are named or numbered and that the system of naming or numbering is *exactly* the same on the picture or file *and* in the text. Remember, the typesetter is not familiar with your book, and he is not going to be able to figure out which images go where without very specific guidance from you.

One other issue regarding pictures, which doesn't really belong here, because it's not about style; but it is very important. If you are using images, make sure that you have the right to use those images. For example, if you resolve to use a full-page illustration by a prominent living artist without getting his permission, you are making a very bad decision. If you want to use a photograph you took of a model, and she never signed a release, better contact her now and get her to sign that release. This stuff can be sticky; call if you have questions and we will offer guidance.

STYLE

Matters of style should, for the most part, follow *The Chicago Manual of Style*, fourteenth edition, and *Webster's Collegiate*

Dictionary, tenth edition. Be consistent in all matters of style and spelling. Make a style sheet in which you resolve all questions of style and spelling, such as names (which should be fact-checked) or words that are not in the dictionary (e.g., technical terms or terminology particular to your subject). Turn in this style sheet with the manuscript so we can bene-fit from it.

Keep to the agreed-upon page count for the book. Please ask any questions you may have, since the ultimate produc-tion of the book will be greatly aided by following these guidelines.

SOME GENERAL MATTERS OF STYLE

- Paragraphs should rarely run longer than half a page.
- Make sure that the table of contents matches the text. Often the chapter titles appear one way in the contents and another in the chapter itself (the same goes for subheads).
- Always use the serial comma—that is, for items in a series, always put a comma after the last item before "and" or "or" (e.g., A, B, and C).
- Em dashes should have no spaces on either side (e.g., fish—small, medium, and large). If you have not created a shortcut key in order to insert em dashes, please use a double dash--which will convert easily to a proper em dash.
- There is no space before or after a forward slash.
- Watch for which/that confusion.
- Watch for noun/pronoun agreement (e.g., do not refer to a company as "them" or use "they" when referring to one person). In cases of political correctness with regard to gender, try to alternate examples from paragraph to paragraph or from case to case (it is often a good idea to assign genders to particular hypothetical examples and use them consistently throughout the manuscript—"the musician" is consistently referred to as "he," "the lawyer" is consistently referred to as "she," and so on).

- Always spell out the word "and" in running text (and even in bulleted lists), unless it is the case that an ampersand appears as a part of a company's legitimate name.
- Spell out the word "versus" unless citing a legal case.
- The words "street," "avenue," "boulevard," or "suite" should be spelled out in addresses.

CHAPTERS AND SUBHEADS

- Chapter titles and all levels of subheads should be in title case (i.e., have initial letters of each word capitalized, except for articles, prepositions, and connectives). The first letter of the first and last word should always be capitalized.
- Don't start chapters with subheads. The first subhead should always follow a block of text introducing the chapter.
- When referring to another chapter in the book, use numerals for the chapter numbers and do not capitalize the word "chapter" (e.g., see chapter 14). The same goes for appendixes (e.g., appendix B). Cross-references between chapters should be filled in when the manuscript is handed in.

LISTS AND TEXT BOXES

- Use text boxes sparingly, if necessary. Usually, material can be organized by being separated into paragraphs and divided with A- or B-heads. Stories, examples, checklists, and forms lend themselves to boxes and "sidebars." These should not be less than seventy-five words or more than a book page, and never more than a two-page spread.
- If you wish to box certain text, indicate this in the manuscript by typing **[begin box]** at the start of the box, and **[end box]** where it concludes. Text in a box should be able to stand by itself and should not be fixed as to where it falls in the chapter.
- Avoid long lists.
- For short lists, use bullets—but try not to do so often. A short bulleted list is often better run together as a paragraph.

- Only number lists if the numbering makes the list easier to understand (such as with a series of steps to be taken). If you are numbering, do not then use lettering for a later list.
- The first letter of a list item is always capitalized, even if the list is a grammatical continuation of the introductory sentence.
- If the reader might want to check off items, it is possible to make checklists by using boxes that can be checked rather than bullets.

Fact Checking

We do not have a fact-checking department. Although our copyeditors and proofreaders do a valiant job of double-checking, you are ultimately responsible for making sure that dates are correct, names and foreign words are spelled correctly, images are properly captioned, credited, cropped, and aligned, and so on.

It would be wise to follow these guidelines even if you are publishing your own book. You, as a publisher as well as an author, have more responsibilities than you would have as an author alone. And if you need to send your manuscript out to a designer or typesetter, your preparation will help him convert your manuscript into book form with greater ease.

The Publisher's Responsibility

- To provide qualified editing and guidance
- To produce a professional-quality book
- To publish your book when promised
- To listen to and value your point of view
- To pay your advance and royalties in a timely manner

Many of these issues will have been addressed in the agreement you signed with your publisher. See chapter 14, The Publishing Agreement.

THE PUBLISHING PROCESS

There are good reasons that it takes so long between the signing of the publishing agreement and the time your book actually appears in bookstores. Your manuscript goes through many hands before it turns into a book. In a large publishing house, it can go through an acquisitions editor, a development editor, a copyeditor, a designer, and one or more proofreaders. Small book publishers may have only one editor.

The following are some of the steps involved in the process of producing a bound book.

1. The manuscript goes to the developmental, or substantive editor, who reads it and makes suggestions and changes—sometimes fairly significant ones—regarding the form and content of the book.
2. The edited manuscript is returned to the author for her review of the changes and, if necessary, for supplying additional copy. There could be more than one round of this type of editing.
3. The manuscript is returned to the editor for review, and then may be turned over to a copyeditor, who will be expected to read the content, focusing mostly on grammar, style, facts, inconsistencies, etc.
4. The manuscript is returned to the author, for review of copy editor's queries and changes.
5. The book cover is designed and approved.
6. The book's interior is designed and sample pages are typeset.
7. The page design is reviewed.
8. When all the edits have been made and the design has been approved, the final typesetting is done.
9. A set of proofs of the typeset book is sent to the author for review.
10. Sets of uncorrected proofs are sent to potential reviewers, and, if there are going to be endorsements on the back cover, the proofs are also sent out to the potential "blurbers."
11. Any needed corrections are done and the final pages are sent to the printer.
12. The back, front, and spine of the cover of the book are finalized.

13. The printer submits "bluelines," or final proofs, to the publisher for final approval.
14. The printer supplies "f & g"s; that is a set of folded and gathered, but unbound pages for the publisher's approval.
15. The printed pages are bound into a book.
16. The books are shipped from the printer to warehouse, or directly to the publisher. From there they will be distributed to bookstores, and wherever else the marketing efforts of the author and the publishing company have managed to place them.

All along the way, there are decisions and choices to be made. In a large publishing company, these decisions are often made in committee. Small publishers will have fewer people evaluating the content and design of the book and can often get a book into print faster than a major publisher.

Here I've really only addressed the editorial part of the publishing process. It will, of course, be your responsibility, as well as the publisher's, to get the finished book out there, through publicity, marketing, and sales.

Chapter 18

Publishing Your Own Book

A person who publishes a book willfully appears before the populace with his pants down. . . . If it is a good book nothing can hurt him. If it is a bad book nothing can help him.

—EDNA ST. VINCENT MILLAY

No agent? No publisher? No problem. Well, maybe no problem. It depends on what your goals are. Many people have self-published, learning how to produce, promote, and market their books. As both author and publisher, those who choose to go this route could have a greater return on sales than they otherwise would have. Once you have completed the research for the Marketing Potential section of your book proposal, you should have a pretty good idea of where your book will sell.

Among my clients are authors who are producing books with no plans to take them to traditional publishers. They already know where and how to sell them. Some have already done so. One of these entrepreneurs is an English teacher who wrote a book about the various fields of writing with an explanation of what is involved in each one. He self-published it with a print run of 5,000 and sold out his first edition within a year or so, marketing it to home-schooling programs.

Another successful self-publisher is a woman who writes a weekly column for a major newspaper, in the form of questions and answers on homeowner associations. She put her articles into a book and sold the book to condominium and cooperative associations as well as to individuals who live in such communities. She is an authority on the subject and her book is always in demand. She sold all 12,000 copies of her first edition within two years and is preparing a second edition.

The owner of an "angel store," a retail gift shop that specializes in all kinds of objects having to do with angels, from knickknacks and jewelry to paintings and books, decided to write and self-publish his own book. He ordered a print run of 5,000 and, selling out within two years, printed a revised edition and had twice the number of books printed because he knew he would eventually sell them all. They were sold not only in his own store but in angel stores throughout the country.

Many authors have done very well with their self-published books. Patricia Fry has written at least a dozen books, some published by established book publishers, some she published herself. She chose to self-publish her book on Ojai, California, history. As a fifth-generation Ojai native, she knew a great deal about this charming little town in a valley about fifteen miles from the Pacific Ocean. She researched its history, gathered 230 old photographs, and published a 300-page book that she titled *The Ojai Valley: An Illustrated History.* She had never published her own book before but she certainly knew what she was doing. She spoke frequently at the local museum and sold her books to bookstores in Ojai and surrounding communities, calling on bookstore owners personally. The book has sold regularly to both local residents and to tourists for years. It is carried in bookstores, gift shops, libraries, and museums not only in Ojai and the nearby communities of Ventura and Santa Barbara but throughout the country. When she sold out of her original books, she published a revised edition. Each time she recouped all of her expenses and began to make a profit within the first few months of publication.

If you decide to produce your book so that it has a professionally published look, you can certainly do so. Hundreds of thousands of authors have self-published. And while most of them have not earned back their costs, many self-publishers have been very successful.

Not all writers' goals are to make a living as a writer or even to earn any money through their writing. Many writers have things they want to write about and maybe even to turn into a book with no desire or expectation of selling it. Like many people, I plan to write my memoirs as a self-healing project as well as a family history to leave to my children and granddaughter. Even if they don't read it until many years from now, someday they will probably want to, and it will be my parting gift to them. Many people want to record their family recipes that have been passed down from generation to generation. Their cookbooks may find a wide readership but even if they don't, most people have parents, aunts, uncles, cousins, children, and grandchildren who would treasure such a book. In some large extended families, this group could account for a hundred or more books.

Self-publishing goes back a long way. Mark Twain was a self-publisher. So were Zane Grey, Walt Whitman, Henry David Thoreau, Edgar Allen Poe, Rudyard Kipling, and Mary Baker Eddy.

Dan Poynter, who has written the definitive book on self-publishing, "fell into publishing," he says. He wrote a technical treatise on the parachute and, unable to get a publisher interested, he went directly to a printer. When the orders poured in, he became a publisher. In 1973 he wrote and published a book on hang gliding and sold over 130,000 copies. His perennially best-selling book, *The Self-Publishing Manual,* is in its thirteenth edition.

Publishing a book isn't as complicated as it may seem and it doesn't have to be outrageously expensive. Many authors publish their own books even if they plan to find a publisher for it later. Very often it is easier to convince a publisher to take your book once they see it in book form and know that you have already sold a number of copies.

SETTING UP A PUBLISHING COMPANY

Setting up a publishing company can be done without having to consult an attorney. Once you have decided on a name for your publishing company you must file the DBA (Doing Business As) with your county, checking their records to be sure that the name is not already in use. You will then have to publish the DBA in a local newspaper for a period of time. To sell your books, you'll need a sales tax permit, which you can get from your state's Board of Equalization. Some cities require a business license. Check with your state's and city's local government offices regarding their requirements. If you have a tax accountant, you should check with him regarding any state and federal tax matters you might want or need to consider, such as paying taxes on the profits or taking a tax write-off for expenses.

GETTING AND FILLING OUT THE PUBLISHING FORMS

You will need to purchase a block of at least ten ISBNs (International Standard Book Numbers). You should also get your copyright registered. Although registration is not required to place the copyright symbol © before your name, registering your copyright offers you certain legal protections that are explained in chapter 9. You will need an LCCN (Library of Congress Card Number) but there is no charge for this. You should complete an "Advance Book Information" form so that your book will be listed in the databases "Books in Print" and "Forthcoming Books" that provide information to bookstores and libraries. You will also need a bar code if you plan to sell your books through retail establishments such as bookstores and gift shops. Usually your printer will provide this for a minimal cost.

These forms need to be completed and submitted in a specific order. For example, you'll need your ISBN before you can apply for your LCCN. You'll have to have your ISBN and your LCCN to apply for your CIP (Cataloguing-in-Publication).

Following is a list of the forms with a brief explanation of each one.

COPYRIGHT REGISTRATION

See chapter 9.

ISBN (International Standard Book Number) Application Form

An ISBN is used for both ordering and cataloging purposes. It is a book's unique identification number. To get forms, write to ISBN, 121 Chanlon Road, New Providence, NJ 07974, call (877) 310-7333, or download them from its Web site. You will receive 10 numbers for a fee of $225 (as of April 2001). Add $50 for priority processing. You can apply online if you charge it to a credit card. To download the forms or apply online, go to *www.bowker.com* or *www.isbn.org.*

Advance Book Information

Fill this out to be listed in the databases, *Forthcoming Books* and *Books in Print,* that are used by libraries and bookstores. You can get this form from R. R. Bowker Data Collection Center, P.O. Box 6000, Oldsmar, FL 34677-6800.

Bar Code

Check with your printer. They usually handle this at the time of printing your book. If not, you can order one from Bar Code Graphics. The e-mail address is sales@barcode-us.com. It will probably cost anywhere from $15 to $30.

Library of Congress Card Number (LCCN)

Write to Library of Congress, Cataloging in Publication Division, 101 Independence Avenue, SE, Washington, DC 20540-4320 and ask for a form called "Request for Preassignment of Library of Congress Catalog Card Number." Contact *http://lcweb.loc.gov/faq/catfaq.html* for more information.

Publisher's Cataloging in Publication (PCIP)

Whereas larger publishers get what is called CIP data directly from the Library of Congress, a self-publisher with fewer than ten books will need to purchase PCIP data from Quality Books. Call or write to them for the form at 1003 W. Pines Road, Oregon, IL 61061-9680, phone (815) 732-4450, fax (815) 732-4499. Librarians need this information to process your book. The fee is $40 for regular service (sixty-day turnaround), $60 for thirty-day turnaround, and $85 for ten-day turnaround. Add $7.50 for unconfirmed fax and $12 for confirmed fax. These rates went into effect October 2001.

The book title, LCCN, PCIP, ISBN, as well as the copyright symbol followed by the date of copyright and the author's name, all go on the copyright page in your book (reverse side of your title page). As rates go up from time to time, check with the above for current rates.

THE COSTS INVOLVED IN SELF-PUBLISHING

The major expenses you will need to consider are the costs of editing, proofreading, designing the cover and interior of the book, typesetting, and printing. You should always have someone proofread the typeset pages of your book. If you do not require the services of an editor and you can do the cover and page design and the computer typesetting yourself, you will save yourself those expenses. You could use Microsoft Word to typeset your book, especially if it is straight text without illustrations. Professionals generally use Quark or PageMaker but those programs are expensive to purchase and difficult to use without training. You may need to get the Adobe Acrobat software to convert your document to a Portable Document Format (PDF) so that you can save it on a disk or CD to send to the printer. Although not all printers will ask for the PDF file, short-run digital printers most likely will require it.

PRICING YOUR BOOK

Before your book goes to a printer you'll have to decide on a price. Check other books of a similar nature and size to see how they are priced, then price your book within the range those books are selling for. The disadvantages to pricing your book too low are that you may find it hard to recoup your costs per book and you risk having your book considered worth less than others. The disadvantage to pricing above the market is that it may be passed over for a book with a less expensive price tag.

FINDING A PRINTER

Do not get more books printed than you believe you can sell within a year. Most first-time publishers are lured into printing thousands of books because the cost per book is so much less than it would be if they printed only a hundred. The sad result is they usually end up with most of their books mildewing in a damp basement or garage. If you don't already *know* where and how you will sell a few thousand books, it's best not to print them. You no longer have to print at least 1,000 books as in the past. A digital printer will print short runs of one copy to 500 books for less than offset printers would charge for that amount, if they were to do it, and most traditional offset printers won't print a small number of books.

Here are examples of potential costs. A digital printer might charge about $1,400 to print 500 copies of a 150-page paperback book. When you add the shipping charges, it may come to nearly $1,500. That's just under $3 per book. If you have only 50 books printed, the cost per book might rise to about $5 per book, but the total cost would be only $250. If you chose to have 5,000 of your books printed, you would be better off going to an offset printer and you might pay only $1.60 per book or less. The quality might be better with an offset printer than with a digital printer but not necessarily. The cost could be $8,000 plus shipping, which would add another $200–$300 to the total. That's fine if you are going to sell 5,000 books, but if you don't, that's a lot of money to spend for printing. I advise my clients to have only a few books printed at first—no more than 100. They can then test the market, send out review copies, make changes to improve the book (and there are always things you see later), and gather endorsements that can go into the next printing of the book. If they get some good reviews, orders will start to come in and they will know how many books to print next time. That way they don't have to tie up more money than necessary or find a safe place to store books that may never sell.

SENDING OUT REVIEW COPIES

It is important to send out review copies to influential journals. A good
review in *Library Journal* can generate orders for 1,000 books or more
within the first few weeks of publication. Review books should be sent
out four to six months before the publication date. Following is a list
of some of the reviewers you should send your book to.

Publishers Weekly
Forecasts
245 W. 17th Street
New York, NY 10011-5300

Library Journal
Book Review Editor
245 W. 17th Street
New York, NY 10011-5300

Kirkus Reviews
Library Advance Information
770 Broadway
New York, NY 10003-9597

ALA Booklist
Up Front, Advance Reviews
50 E. Huron Street
Chicago, IL 60611

New York Times Book Review
229 W. 43rd Street
New York, NY 10036

New York Review of Books
1755 Broadway, Floor 5
New York, NY 10019

New York Times
Daily Book Review Section
229 W. 43rd Street
New York, NY 10036

Los Angeles Times Book
Review
202 W. First Street
Los Angeles, CA 90012

School Library Journal
245 W. 17th Street
New York, NY 10011-5300

Choice
Editorial Department
100 Riverview Center
Middletown, CT 06457

Midwest Book Review
278 Orchard Drive
Oregon, WI 53575

Chicago Tribune Books
Book Reviews
435 N. Michigan Ave.
Chicago, IL 60611

Independent Publisher
Jenkins Group
400 W. Front Street, Suite 4A
Traverse City, MI 49684

Newsday
Book Reviews
Two Park Avenue
New York, NY 10016

San Francisco Chronicle
Book Reviews
901 Mission
San Francisco, CA 94103

USA Today
Book Reviews
1000 Wilson Blvd.
Arlington, VA 22229

Washington Post
Book World
1150 15th Street, NW
Washington, DC 10071

If you get a good review in one of the above publications, be prepared to get a lot of attention. Don't be surprised if a book wholesaler contacts you, as the publisher, to place orders of a hundred or more books at a time. In such a case, it will be necessary to sign an agreement with the wholesaler. Many bookstores and libraries will not order directly from a publisher, only through a wholesaler such as Baker & Taylor or Ingram. Major wholesalers expect a discount of 55 percent of the cover price of the book. If you sign with a distributor (from which wholesalers and some bookstores and libraries purchase their books) you will have to give up as much as 65 percent. But it makes sense when you consider that they will be ordering your books by the hundreds or thousands.

There is a great deal of important information you need to know about self-publishing and it can't all be covered in this book. The above is really only an overview. For more detailed information, get Dan Poynter's book, *The Self-Publishing Manual: How to Write, Print, and Sell Your Own Book.* It is published by his company, Para Publishing of Santa Barbara, California.

Self-publishing is exciting and can now be done without your having to mortgage your house or hold up a bank. And you won't know until you've published a book whether you have a best-seller in you. Maybe, just maybe you do.

Chapter 19

Ethics And Legal Concerns

Ignorance of the law excuses no man.

—JOHN SELDEN

Plagiarism, copyright infringement, invasion of privacy, and defamation of character, which includes libel and slander, have no place in a book—or anywhere else for that matter. That isn't a moral judgment. It's just plain common sense. We are judged by what we say and what we do. And it may not matter whether we intentionally and knowingly violated a person's rights, stole his words, or damaged his reputation. We can still be sued.

The written word has great power. Once we have put something in writing and sent it out into the world, we can't hit the delete button and get rid of it. Since there's no changing the past, we must make our corrections in the present, or better yet, learn how to avoid making the mistakes in the first place.

It's more than a matter of ethics; what we write has the potential not only to hurt others but to harm ourselves. Our words can come back to haunt us. Very often writers are unaware that they have violated a person's rights or caused consternation or harm. The laws are so complex it isn't always easy to know when we have broken them. But we can become alert to some of the broad rules, including what the pitfalls may be and where they might lie. The following is an examination of some of the things that can get us into trouble.

DEFAMATION

When you injure a person by saying untrue things about him, you have "defamed" him. Defamation by speaking ill of a person is "slander." When lies about a person are written or broadcast it is considered "libel." The difference between the two terms is somewhat muddy but historically it depends on how wide an audience the defamer reached.

Libel is defamation by written or printed words, pictures, or in any form other than by spoken words and gestures; slander is defamation by oral utterance other than by writing, pictures, etc., according to *Webster's New Universal Unabridged Dictionary.*

Some of the elements that are considered in defamation lawsuits are as follows:

- **Accuracy.** If it is a false statement that does harm to a person, company, or product, it is libelous. If it is true, it's not defamatory.
- **Opinion.** If it is an opinion, not a fact, it is protected under the First Amendment.
- **Publication.** If the false, injurious statement was shared with a third party, it is considered "published" and therefore libelous.
- **Injury.** If the lie caused injury to a person's reputation, personal or professional standing, or caused anguish, it is libelous.

FAIR USE

The owner of copyright has the right to reproduce or to authorize others to reproduce her work. This right, however, is subject to certain limitations. One such limitation is the doctrine of "fair use." A list of the purposes for which the reproduction of a specific work may be considered "fair" is contained in Section 107 of the Copyright Law. Some of them are criticism, comment, news reporting, teaching, and research. In determining whether a use is fair, Section 107 lists four factors to be considered. They are:

1. The purpose and character of the use, including whether such use is of commercial nature or is for nonprofit educational purposes
2. The nature of the copyrighted work
3. The amount and substantiality of the portion used in relation to the copyrighted work as a whole
4. The effect of the use upon the potential market for or value of the copyrighted work

Be aware, however, that the distinction between what is "fair use" and what is infringement cannot be easily defined. Attorney/author Tad Crawford states, "Although everyone who deals with intellectual property seems to have heard of 'fair use,' misconceptions are rife about what the doctrine makes it 'safe' to do."

To quote from Copyright Office FL102 on Fair Use: "There is no specific number of words, lines, or notes that may safely be taken without permission. Acknowledging the source of the copyrighted material does not substitute for obtaining permission."

Generally, authors, scholars, researchers, and educators may quote small portions of a copyrighted work without getting permission or paying a fee. Examples would be a book reviewer quoting excerpts from a new book or a historian quoting certain passages from an existing work for educational purposes. However, fair use is virtually impossible to determine for sure.

The Copyright Office cannot make the determination of whether a certain use may be considered fair. It cannot give you advice regarding possible copyright violations. And it can't give you permission to use any copyrighted material. You must get permission from the copyright owner.

There is more information on this in the third edition of *The Writer's Legal Guide: An Authors Guild Desk Reference,* by Tad Crawford and Kay Murray. The Copyright Office provides information on fair use in Circular 21 and FL102. If your question is not clearly answered in any of those publications, you'd best obtain written permission from the owner of the copyright.

This is another case for the rule, "When in doubt, take it out," until you either have permission or have consulted with a lawyer who has expertise in this area. Unauthorized use of copyrighted material can be punished by heavy damage awards.

Resources

The lists of resources that follow are only a few that are available to authors. There are many valuable publications and organizations that offer specific help. Your goals, needs, specialty and location will determine which ones are right for you.

PUBLICATIONS

Books

Appelbaum, Judith. *How to Get Happily Published: A Complete and Candid Guide.* New York: Harper Perennial, 1998.

Bartlett, John. *Bartlett's Familiar Quotations: A Collection of Passages, Phrases, and Proverbs Traced to Their Sources in Ancient and Modern Literature.* Edited by Justin Kaplan. 17th ed. New York: Little, Brown and Company, 2002.

Books in Print. R. R. Bowker & Co. Published annually.

Bunnin, Brad, and Peter Beren. *The Writer's Legal Companion: The Complete Handbook for the Working Writer.* Reading: Perseus Books, 1998.

The Cambridge Factfinder. Cambridge: Cambridge University Press, 1995.

The Chicago Manual of Style: The Essential Guide for Writers, Editors, and Publishers. 14th ed. Chicago: The University of Chicago Press, 1993.

Crawford, Tad. *Business and Legal Forms for Authors and Self-Publishers.* Rev. ed. New York: Allworth Press, 1999.

Crawford, Tad, and Kay Murray. *The Writer's Legal Guide: An Author's Guild Desk Reference.* New York: Allworth Press, 2002.

Fishman, Stephen, and Patti Gima, eds. *The Copyright Handbook: How to Protect & Use Written Works.* Berkeley: Nolo Press, 1997. Covers all aspects of copyright.

Forthcoming Books. R. R. Bowker & Co. Published annually.

Gordon, Karen Elizabeth. *The Deluxe Transitive Vampire: The Ultimate Handbook of Grammar for the Innocent, the Eager, and the Doomed.* New York: Pantheon Books, 1993. In spite of its odd title, a very useful and interesting book on grammar.

————. *The New Well-Tempered Sentence: A Punctuation Handbook for the Innocent, the Eager, and the Doomed.* New York: Ticknor & Fields, 1993. An entertaining way to learn punctuation.

Guide to Literary Agents. Cincinnati: Writer's Digest Books. Published annually.

Herman, Jeff, and Deborah M. Adams. *Write the Perfect Book Proposal: 10 Proposals That Sold and Why.* New York: John Wiley & Sons, Inc., 2001.

The International Thesaurus of Quotations. New York: HarperPerennial, 1996.

Jassin, Lloyd J., and Steven C. Schechter. *The Copyright Permission and Libel Handbook: A Step-by-Step Guide for Writers, Editors, and Publishers.* New York: John Wiley & Sons, Inc., 1998. Discusses how to clear rights; for those interested in using copyrighted material.

King, Stephen. *On Writing: A Memoir of the Craft.* New York: Pocket Books, 2000.

Kirsch, Jonathan. *Kirsch's Guide to the Book Contract: For Authors, Publishers, Editors and Agents.* Los Angeles: Acrobat Books, 1999.

Lamott, Anne. *Bird by Bird: Some Instructions on Writing and Life.* New York: Anchor Books/Doubleday, 1995.

Larson, Michael. *How to Write a Book Proposal.* Cincinnati: Writer's Digest Books, 1997.

Literary Market Place, R. R. Bowker. Published annually. A directory of the publishing industry that contains a comprehensive list of publishers and publishing-allied groups, such as literary agencies, writers' conferences, wholesalers, and distributors.

Mutchler, John C. *The American Directory of Writer's Guidelines.* Fresno, Calif.: Quill Driver Books, 1998. A compilation for freelancers from more than 1,300 magazine and book publishers.

The New York Public Library Desk Reference. New York: Prentice Hall, 1993. "The complete resource for quick answers to all your questions," according to the publisher. It also contains hundreds of illustrations, tables, charts, and graphs.

The Oxford Dictionary of Quotations. 5th ed. Getty Center for Education in the Arts, 1999.

Poynter, Dan. *The Self-Publishing Manual: How to Write, Print and Sell Your Own Book.* Santa Barbara, Calif.: Para Publishing, 2002.

Roget's Thesaurus of English Words & Phrases. Essex: Longman Group Limited, 1982.

Ross, Marilyn, and Tom Ross. *Jump Start Your Book Sales: A Money-Making Guide for Authors, Independent Publishers and Small Presses.* Buena Vista, Calif.: Communication Creativity, 1999.

Sharpe, Leslie T., and Irene Gunther. *Editing Fact and Fiction: A Concise Guide to Book Editing.* Cambridge: Cambridge University Press. 1995.

Stebel, S. L. *Double Your Creative Power.* Santa Barbara, Calif.: Allen A. Knoll Publishers, 1996.

Strunk, William, Jr., and E. B. White. *The Elements of Style.* Needham Heights, Mass.: Allyn and Bacon, 2000.

Waller, James, ed. *Freelance Writers' Guide.* New York: The National Writers Union, 2000. Provides real-life information about prevailing practices and working conditions, rights, contracts, and more.

The Oxford Dictionary of Quotations. 5th ed. Getty Center for Education in the Arts, 1999.

The Writer's Handbook. Boston: The Writer Inc. Articles on writing and listings of markets and resources. Published annually.

Writer's Market. Cincinnati: Writer's Digest Books. Lists of book and magazine editors who buy what you write. Published annually.

Zinsser, William. *On Writing Well: The Classic Guide to Writing Nonfiction.* New York: HarperPerennial, 1998.

Periodicals

Library Journal. Reed Business Information. Published twenty times a year.

Poets & Writers Magazine. Poets & Writers, Inc. A bimonthly magazine for literary writers and poets.

Publishers Weekly. A Cahners/R. R. Bowker Publication. "The International News Magazine of Book Publishing and Bookselling."

The Writer. Kalmbach Publishing Co. A monthly magazine.

Writer's Digest. F & W Publications. A monthly magazine.

ORGANIZATIONS

Agent Research & Evaluation
334 E. 30th Street
New York, NY 10016
Web site: *www.agentresearch.com*
AR&E tracks agents in court records and the press. They publish a newsletter and sell reports from their database.

American Society of Journalists & Authors, Inc.
1501 Broadway
Suite 302
New York, NY 10036
Phone: (212) 997-0947
Fax: (212) 768-7414
Web site: *www.asja.org*
Dues are $165 per year.

Association of Authors' Representatives (AAR)
10 Astor Place
3rd floor
New York, NY 10003
Phone: (212) 353-3709
Web site: *www.aar-online.org*
Literary agents who are members of AAR subscribe to a code of ethics. Send $7 and SASE with postage for a two-ounce first-class letter for a list of member agents.

The Authors Guild
330 W. 42nd Street
New York, NY 10036
Phone: (212) 563-5904
Fax: (212) 564-8363
Web site: *www.authorsguild.org*
Provides a variety of services, including a quarterly newsletter, a guide to publishing contracts, and health insurance. Dues are $90 per year and include membership in The Authors League of America.

The Authors League of America
330 W. 42nd Street
New York, NY 10036
Phone: (212) 564-8350
A sister organization to The Authors Guild. See above Web site for more information.

National Writers Union, East Coast Office
113 University Place
6th floor
New York, NY 10003
Phone: (212) 254-0279
Fax (212) 254-0673
Web site: *www.nwu.org/nwu*
E-mail: *www.nwu.org/nwu*
A trade union committed to improving the working conditions of

freelance writers. Dues based on writing income start at $90 per year.

National Writers Union, West Coast Office
337 W. 17th Street
Suite 101
Oakland, CA 94612
Phone: (510) 839-0110
Fax: (510) 839-6097
Web site: see previous entry

PEN American Center
568 Broadway
New York, NY 10012
Phone: (212) 334-1660
Fax: (212) 334-2181
Web site: *www.pen.org*
The largest of 124 centers worldwide. Membership consists of playwrights, essayists, editors, and novelists.

Publishers Marketing Association (PMA)
627 Aviation Way
Manhattan Beach, CA 90266
Web site: *www.pma.online.org*
A trade association for small publishers offering educational, marketing, and direct mail programs.

Science Fiction & Fantasy Writers of America, Inc.
532 La Guardia Place #632
New York, NY 10012-1428
Web site: *www.sfwa.org*
They have a tutorial of what to look for in an agent, a model agent contract, case studies, and a list of resources.

Small Press Center for Independent Publishing
20 W. 44th Street
New York, NY 10036
Phone: (212) 764-7021
Web site: *www.smallpress.org*
Nonprofit cultural and educational institution dedicated to promoting interaction between the public and small independent book publishers.

Small Publishers, Artists & Writers Network (SPAWN)
P.O. Box 2653
Ventura, CA 93002-2653
Phone/fax: (805) 643-2403
Web site: *www.spawn.org*
A nonprofit educational organization formed to "provide information, resources and a supportive networking environment for artists, writers, and other creative people interested in the publishing process."

Small Publishers Association of North America (SPAN)
P.O. Box 1306
425 Cedar Street
Buena Vista, CO 81211-1306
Web site: *www.spannet.org*
A trade association for small publishers offering education and marketing opportunities.

Writers Guild of America—East
555 W. 57th St.
New York, NY 10019
Phone: (212) 767-7800
Fax: (212) 582-1909
Web site: *www.wgaeast.org*
A labor union representing professional writers in motion pictures, television, and radio. Members must be published or employed in the field.

Writers Guild of America—West
8955 Beverly Blvd.
West Hollywood, CA 90048
Phone: (213) 550-1000
Web site: *www.wga.org*
Provides a list of WGA signatory agents for $2 and SASE sent to Agency Department. Both WGAE and WGAW provide a registration service for literary material.

Glossary

acknowledgment   an expression of appreciation

acquisitions editor   the person at a book publishing company in charge of acquiring product; usually the person to whom a query or book proposal is sent

active voice   a voice of verbal inflection in which the subject of the sentence is represented as performing the action expressed by the verb: *She will always remember her first love; he hit the ball.*

adjective   any of a class of words used to modify a noun by limiting, qualifying, or specifying. It is distinguished by having comparative and superlative endings like *-able, -ous, -er, -est.* An adjective describes or specifies the quantity or quality of.

advance   money paid to an author by a publisher prior to publication. An advance is paid against royalties.

adverb   any of a class of words distinguished by the ending *-ly* or by functioning as a modifier of verbs or clauses, adjectives, or other adverbs or adverbial phrases, as *very, well, quickly*

agent   a person authorized to act on another's behalf. Agents are paid on a percentage basis. Literary agents working with authors of books usually get 15 percent; script agents who work with scriptwriters usually get 10 percent.

almanac   an annual reference book of useful and interesting facts

analogy   a similarity between like features of two things, a comparison; usually followed by *to, with, or between*

antagonist   a major character opposing the protagonist

back matter   elements of a book that follow the text, such as appendix, index, glossary, list of resources, bibliography, and author biography

bar code   a set of short, vertical lines and spaces printed on a product, designed to be machine readable to yield a price, ISBN, etc.; required by most retailers

best-seller   book that sells in large quantities; based on sales by bookstores, wholesalers, and/or distributors

bibliography   a list of source materials such as books and articles used in the preparation of a book or referred to in the text

binding   pages of a book bound together with thread, staples, adhesive, or other means

blueline   (also called blues) a paper print made from a single negative, used primarily as a proof, to check content and/or positioning

book review   a critical appraisal of a book often reflecting a reviewer's personal opinion and/or recommendation

Books in Print   listings of books currently in print, published by R. R. Bowker, providing ordering information including titles, authors, publishers, ISBNs, binding (hardcover or paperback), and prices

bundle of rights   a copyright that provides authors, music composers, and creators of artistic works the sole right to grant or refuse permission to use their copyrighted works

case bound   book bound in a rigid material; also known as hardcover

casing   alternate term for binding

character   a person represented in a story, drama, etc.

CIP   Cataloging-in-Publication: a cataloging record prepared to the standards of the Library of Congress which enables libraries to catalog titles

cliché   a trite, stereotyped expression; a platitude

coauthor   one of two or more joint authors; to write in joint authorship

collaboration   working with one another; cooperation; as writers collaborating to produce a book

comb binding   mechanical binding using a plastic spring-like comb that fits through holes punched in the edges of pages

concept   a general notion or idea

consistency   adherence to the same principles, course, or form; uniformity

content editor   person who evaluates the flow, logic, and overall message of a manuscript

continuity   a continuous or connected whole

copyeditor person who does line-by-line editing to correct errors in spelling, grammar, consistency, punctuation, etc.

copyright a legal right granted to an author, composer, or artist for exclusive publication, production, sale, or distribution of a literary, musical, or artistic work for a specified period of time

cover letter a brief explanatory letter that accompanies a manuscript or book proposal

deadline author's due date for delivery of the completed manuscript to the publisher

defamation false or unjustified injury of another's good reputation, as by slander or libel

desktop publishing creating and composing pages comprised of text and graphics on a computer

distributor a firm that stocks, promotes, sells, and distributes materials

dust jacket a printed wrapper, usually paper, placed around a case-bound book

edit to revise or correct, as a manuscript

editor a person who edits material for a publication; a manager or supervisor for a publication such as a book publishing company, newspaper, or magazine (see *copyeditor* and *content editor*)

electronic publishing the process of using a computer to enter both text and graphics and to integrate them for final output

endpapers the pages at the beginning and end of a book that are pasted against the inside board of the case; also called endleaves or lining paper

ethics moral principles or values

ethnic characteristic of a people or group sharing a common and distinctive culture, religion, or language

fiction the class of literature comprising works of imaginative narration

flow to proceed continuously, smoothly, or easily

flyleaf a blank page at the beginning or end of a book

font a complete assortment of type of one style and size

foreword part of the front matter of a book; a short introductory statement usually written by someone other than the author, often an authority on the subject of the book

format the general appearance of a book such as typeface, margins, binding, etc.

front matter the elements that precede the text of a book, such as the title page, copyright page, dedication, table of contents, foreword, preface, introduction, and acknowledgments

galley   printed proof of text copy before being made into pages, often used for proofreading or presentation reviews

genre   a class or category of artistic endeavor having a particular form, content, technique, or the like

ghostwriter   a person who writes for another person who is presumed to be the author

gutter   inner margin of each page, from printing to binding

hardcover   book bound in a rigid material; also known as case bound

idiomatic   peculiar to or characteristic of a particular language or dialect: *idiomatic expression;* having a distinctive style, esp. in the arts: *idiomatic writing*

infringement   a violation as of a law or agreement

Internet   an interconnected system of networks that connects computers around the world

introduction   a preliminary part of a book leading up to the main part and written by the author; may be extensive and is usually printed as part of the text

ISBN   International Standard Book Number: the International standard numbering system for the information industry; required for books sold through bookstores

jargon   specialized language of a trade, profession, or similar group

libel   a defamatory statement

LCCN   Library of Congress Card Number: a preassigned card number issued by the Library of Congress. A unique identification number assigned to the catalog record created for each book in its catalogued collections

Library of Congress   one of the major library collections in the world, located in Washington, D.C., and functioning as the national library of the United States though not officially designated as such

license   official or legal permission to do or own a specified thing

Literary Market Place (LMP)   annual directory of the publishing industry

margins   the unprinted space between the text and the edge of the page

metaphor   a figure of speech in which a term or phrase is applied to something to which it is not literally applicable in order to suggest a resemblance

narrative   a story or account of events, experiences, or the like, whether true or fictitious

nonfiction   all writing or books not fiction, poetry, or drama; the broadest category of written works

noun   any member of a class of words that can function as the main or only elements of subjects or objects. Nouns refer to persons, places, things, states, or qualities.

novel   a fictitious prose narrative of considerable length and complexity, portraying characters and presenting a sequential organization of action and scenes

paperback   a book with a flexible paper binding

PCIP   Publisher's Cataloging in Publication; a service of Quality Books Inc. Provides librarians with information needed to determine shelf location in libraries

passive voice   a voice of verbal inflection in which the subject of the sentence is the object of the action rather than causing the action: *The ball was hit by him.*

perfect bound   the binding usually used on a paperback book where the cover is glued into place

person   in grammar, a category used to distinguish between the speaker of an utterance and those to or about whom he is speaking. In English there are three persons in the pronouns: first person, *I* and *we*; second person, *you;* third person, *he, she, it, they*

plagiarism   the unauthorized use of the language and thoughts of another author and representing them as one's own work

plot   also called storyline; the plan or main story of a novel or short story

preface   the author's own statement, often including acknowledgments. It follows the foreword if there is one and is part of the front matter of a book.

proofread   to read and mark corrections in a manuscript or galley

protagonist   the leading character

public domain   published material that is available for use without the need to obtain permission, either because it has not been copyrighted or has a copyright that has expired

publisher   the company or entity that prepares printed material for public distribution or sale

punctuation   the use of standard signs and marks in writing to separate words into sentences, clauses, and phrases in order to clarify meaning

query letter   a letter, usually no more than one-page long, in which a writer proposes an article or book idea; written to an agent or publisher asking for either representation or publication of the author's writing

saddle stitch   a binding that fastens pages together with wires (resembling staples) through the middle fold of the sheets

SASE   self-addressed stamped envelope

simile   a figure of speech in which two unlike things are explicitly compared

spine   the back of a bound book connecting the front and back covers; also called backbone

spiral bound   a type of mechanical binding using a continuous wire of corkscrew or spring coil form that runs through holes punched in the binding edge

story   narration of an event or series of events

synopsis   a general view; a brief narrative description of the book, usually one or two pages in length

tense   a set of tense forms indicating a particular time. Example: past tense, *I saw the painting;* present tense, *I see the painting;* future tense, *I will see the painting*

theme   an idea, point of view, or perception

thesaurus   a book of synonyms and antonyms

transition   passage from one subject to another

treatment   in screenwriting, a synopsized narration of the story, action, and dialogue; usually containing more pages than a synopsis for a book

trim size   the finished size of a book after trimming

verb   part of speech that expresses action, existence, or occurrence

wholesaler   a company that takes orders, buys from publishers or distributors, and sells to retailers

word wrap   also called wraparound: a word processing feature that automatically spills text from one line to the next without manually inserting line returns

Index

BOOKS FROM ALLWORTH PRESS

Writing.com: Creative Internet Strategies to Advance Your Writing Career, Revised Edition
by Moira Allen (paperback, 6 × 9, 256 pages, $19.95)

The Writer's Guide to Queries, Pitches, and Proposals
by Moira Allen (paperback, 6 × 9, 288 pages, $16.95)

Making Crime Pay: The Writer's Guide to Criminal Law, Evidence, and Procedure
by Andrea Campbell (paperback, 6 × 9, 304 pages, $19.95)

The Journalist's Craft: A Guide to Writing Better Stories
edited by Dennis Jackson and John Sweeney (paperback, 6 × 9, 256 pages, $19.95)

The Writer's Legal Guide: An Authors Guild Desk Reference, Third Edition
by Tad Crawford and Kay Murray (paperback, 6 × 9, 320 pages, $19.95)

Business and Legal Forms for Authors and Self-Publishers, Revised Edition
by Tad Crawford (paperback, 8½ × 11, 192 pages, includes CD-ROM, $22.95)

The Copyright Guide: A Friendly Guide for Protecting and Profiting from Trademarks
by Lee Wilson (paperback, 6 × 9, 208 pages, $19.95)

Marketing Strategies for Writers
by Michael Sedge (paperback, 6 × 9, 224 pages, $16.95)

Writing for Interactive Media: The Complete Guide
by Jon Samsel and Darryl Wimberly (paperback, 6 × 9, 320 pages, $19.95)

The Writer's Guide to Corporate Communications
by Mary Moreno (paperback, 6 × 9, 192 pages, $19.95)

Writing Scripts Hollywood Will Love, Revised Edition
by Katherine Atwell Herbert (paperback, 6 × 9, 160 pages, $14.95)

So You Want to Be a Screenwriter: How to Face the Fears and Take the Risks
by Sara Caldwell and Marie-Eve Kielson (paperback, 6 × 9, 224 pages, $14.95)

The Screenwriter's Guide to Agents and Managers
by John Scott Lewinski (paperback, 6 × 9, 256 pages, $18.95)

The Screenwriter's Legal Guide, Second Edition
by Stephen F. Breimer (paperback, 6 × 9, 320 pages, $19.95)

Please write to request our free catalog. To order by credit card, call 1-800-491-2808 or send a check or money order to Allworth Press, 10 East 23rd Street, Suite 510, New York, NY 10010. Include $5 for shipping and handling for the first book ordered and $1 for each additional book. Ten dollars plus $1 for each additional book if ordering from Canada. New York State residents must add sales tax.

To see our complete catalog on the World Wide Web, or to order online, you can find us at *www.allworth.com*.